Origins of Instability in Early Republican Mexico

Origins of Instability

in Early Republican Mexico

Donald Fithian Stevens

Duke University Press
Durham and London 1991

Library of Congress Cataloging-in-Publication Data
appear on the last printed page of this book.
Chapter 2 was originally published as "Economic Fluctuations and Political Instability in Early Republican Mexico," *The Journal of Interdisciplinary History* 16 (1986): 645–665, and is reprinted with revisions with the
permission of the editors of the journal and the MIT Press, Cambridge,
Massachusetts, © 1986 by the Massachusetts Institute of Technology and
the editors of *The Journal of Interdisciplinary History.* An earlier version of
chapter 7 appeared in *La ciudad, el campo y la frontera en la historia de
México,* 2 vols., ed. Ricardo A. Sánchez Flores, Eric Van Young, Gisela
von Wobesar, (Mexico: Instituto des Investigaciones Historicas, Universidad Nacional Autónoma de México, 1991).

In memory of my father,

George Tomlinson Stevens,

and in gratitude to my mother,

Bernice Brand Stevens

Contents

Tables and Figure

Acknowledgments

This book had its origins in a dissertation, and before that, in a seminar paper, and before that in a methodology course, all directed by John H. Coatsworth. His training in the quantitative approach to history gave me the tools to work on these problems. I am profoundly grateful for his criticism and his support during a decade of research, writing, and rewriting. I hope that those who know the work of Friedrich Katz will find the imprint of his training on these pages as well, particularly in regard to regional social variation. The magnitude of his kindness is well-known to all who have enjoyed the privilege of working with him. I am also grateful to Frank Safford, who read the dissertation on short notice; his extensive and insightful comments led to many improvements. Without the encouragement and guidance of Barbara A. Tenenbaum, I might never have attempted this project, or might never have become a historian. Her teaching inspired me to study Latin America and nineteenth-century Mexico.

Dra. Josefina Vázquez, Director of the Centro de Estudios Históricos at El Colegio de México, welcomed me for a term there as an *investigador visitante*. Since then, she has read several portions of the manuscript and provided invaluable criticism. Edith Couturier, Charles A. Hale, Hugh H. Hamill, Lyman L. Johnson, John E. Kicza, Douglas V. Porpora, Robert A. Potash, Peter H. Smith, John Tutino, Eric Van Young, Stuart Voss, Mark Wasserman, and David J. Weber have also commented on various portions of the manuscript as it evolved. I am delighted to acknowledge their help. Timothy E. Anna and Richard J. Salvucci read and reread the entire manuscript. I owe each of them a debt of unquantifiable magnitude.

Research funding was provided by the Henry L. and Grace Doherty Charitable Foundation and the Organization of American States. The University of Chicago History Department and Latin American Studies Center and the College of Arts and Sciences of Drexel University provided computer time and travel funds. Without the support of Thomas L. Canavan, Dean of the College of Arts and Sciences, and Philip V. Cannistraro and Eric Dorn Brose as Heads of the Department of History and Politics at Drexel I could not have completed this project. Patricia Cooper has also been both an inspiration and a friend.

I have relied on librarians and computer experts to a greater degree than most historians. In Mexico, staff of the Biblioteca Nacional and the Colegio's Centro de Computación provided exceptional service. I am especially grateful to Leonor Herández and Francisco Durán. The University of Chicago Interlibrary Loan never failed to locate obscure volumes quickly and cheerfully. The staff of the University of Chicago computer center miraculously decoded the data on the tape I brought back from Mexico. Elizabeth Davis and Art MacMahon of Drexel's Office of Computing Services worked hard to make the transition to yet another computer seem effortless. Richard Binder, María Silva Kuhn, and the Interlibrary Loan staff of the Drexel Library deserve special mention as well.

Over the course of this project I have accumulated friends whose contributions to this project are as much personal as professional, but without any one of them the effort might have been derailed. Linda Arnold, Antonio Diez, Carlos Esquivel, Flor Garduño, Nancy González, David Hartman, Miren Izavrieta, David Stevens, and David and Graciela Walker all made immeasurable contributions during the research stage. Most of all, I am grateful to Judith Silver, who has become an indispensable and cherished partner.

The reader might well wonder, given the vast quantity and high quality of assistance I have received in the course of completing this project, why it is not a better, or at least a longer, book. Its brevity, as well as its shortcomings, are entirely my responsibility.

One

Instability and

History

Independence transformed Mexico from Spain's largest and most prosperous colony to a sovereign nation suffering economic decline and political strife. Historical writing on early republican Mexico has emphasized the new nation's weakness: the loss of Texas in 1836, the "Pastry War" with France in 1838, and, most dramatically, the loss of half its national territory to the United States in the War of 1846–1848. The reasons for the rapid transition from a strong, stable colony to a weak, unstable nation remain poorly understood. Nearly twenty years ago Josefina Vázquez wrote that "Mexican historiography has forgotten the entire period from 1821 to 1855 almost systematically."[1] Neglect, she suggested, resulted from the complexity and gloominess of an age universally regarded as a blot on the national record. The promise of independence was not fulfilled; Mexican politicians fought among themselves while the United States grabbed the northern half of the new nation. Mexico suffered economic decline as well as political reverses. While the United States industrialized, the Mexican economy faltered. John Coatsworth has estimated that most of the difference in economic productivity between the United States and Mexico can be attributed to nineteenth-century political instability.[2] In the words of Edmundo O'Gorman, the period presents

> a spectacle of unspeakable sadness: . . . a tedious rosary of *pronunciamientos* and *golpes de Estado* which seems to demon-

strate nothing more than the congenital incapacity of our people to govern themselves and to establish the basis of a civilized life together. That, in effect, has been and continues to be an interpretation much touted as true by foreign historiographers and one that finds adherents even today among our resentful and less intelligent reactionaries.[3]

These observations may be less true now than they were in the 1950s and 1960s. Scholars in Mexico, Europe, and the United States have made notable contributions in these last decades, adding to our understanding of this crucial period in Mexico's history.[4] But the central problem of the era, the collapse of stable government, remains largely unexplained. All too often historians retreat to outdated historiographical notions to simplify the explanation of Mexico's political instability. Antonio López de Santa Anna, president of Mexico on eleven distinct occasions, has been the principal scapegoat for the trials of the young nation. One man's flawed character has been blamed for Mexico's problems, as if Santa Anna's personal weaknesses infected the entire nation.[5]

The contagion has been called caudillismo. Social scientists have developed a series of hypotheses to explain the contrast between the immediately apparent struggles for power and the more intangible foundations of political conflict. The caudillo thesis discounts political motivations and regards caudillos as unprincipled opportunists who mimicked political discourse to hide personal ambitions. This emphasis on caudillismo illustrates the degree to which historical writing on this period has rested on biography, and on the biography of this one man in particular. As Moisés González Navarro noted, Mexican historiography has "suffered from the inconvenience of explaining Mexico in terms of Santa Anna rather than Santa Anna in terms of Mexico."[6]

In early republican Mexico politicians gained and lost power with bewildering rapidity. Traditional political history has been unable to encompass the complexities of this turbulence. The lack of consensus among historians about the roots of instability in these years can be traced to the inadequacies of the traditional historical method of archival research when applied to this problem. Historians tend toward the study of decision-making in stable polities and toward the study of "meaningful" conflicts that can be termed revolutions or civil wars. Instability falls between these two cases. It presents unusual problems for the historian in that it is neither stable nor apparently significant. Yet these judgments tell us more about the methodological biases of qualitative historical research than about the nature of instability. Analyses of decision-making and policy formation are suited to stable periods when institutions behave with some consistency and decision-making processes can be studied on the basis of evidence preserved in archives. Traditional analysis introduces its own characteristic biases and assumptions,[7] but the traditional historical method presents further difficulties specific to periods of instability. For unstable periods it is hard to generalize on the basis of decisions since administrations were brief and decisions were not enforced or were quickly reversed. In this period of Mexican history the most important political decisions were often to replace cabinet ministers or overthrow a government; but the result has been considered merely rotation, not revolution.

By accepted standards, revolution occurs very infrequently in Latin America, and historians have been reluctant to apply the term to early republican Mexican history.[8] Few authorities recognize even the possibility of social revolution in this period. On the contrary, political motives have been heavily discounted. Political positions were mere affectations, and personalism and opportunism outweighed ideology. Many writers argue that there was no drastic social or economic change because politicians did not want change; they only wanted to sack the treasury.

The obstacles to historical studies of instability are considerable. Instability appears to be a paradoxical concept. It signifies considerable motion without much movement in any direction for very long—hyperkinesis combined with apparent stasis. The visibility of these struggles to occupy government posts contrasts with the more obscure motivations for political conflict. A constantly changing cast of political actors makes it difficult to analyze those policy decisions that are made and the power exercised in enforcing them. The frequency of forced resignations of presidents and changes in the compositions of cabinets makes the assumption of the generality of power even more questionable. When politicians cannot maintain themselves in the hierarchy, how much power can their policy decisions express?

There is a further paradox. On one hand, there are considerable theoretical and practical obstacles to the study of instability. On the other, there is no shortage of explanations for Mexico's postindependence instability; there are rather too many distinct and contradictory hypotheses. Perhaps instability was caused primarily by short-term economic and fiscal changes, in which case political differences may be superfluous; or instability was chiefly the result of intractable political conflicts that were rooted in long-term social and economic differences. Instability might have resulted from a lack of political experience, or from politicians with inappropriate social backgrounds or inadequate socialization, or from programs and policies ill-suited to Mexico's independent political situation.

Examples can be cited to support each explanation. An empty national treasury apparently coincided with the inability of politicians to hold power for very long. Yet at the same time, radical artisans and provincial leaders armed the masses to attack armories and government offices. Evidence to support such divergent, if not contradictory, hypotheses might be considered proof of a complex and multifaceted explanation, but selected examples are never a substitute for systematic testing of a hypothesis. In a period when almost every conceivable incident and alignment actually happened at least once, we should not be surprised that multiple examples might be found to support any sort of explanation. Hypotheses have proliferated in the absence of systematic empirical studies.

Given the limitations and inherent biases of traditional historical research, the temptation is strong to focus on those brief interludes of relative calm in this confounding muddle. In fact, much of the best historical writing on the early republic occupies these precarious niches. We have two major studies of the relatively stable 1820s.[9] Much of the best research in early nineteenth-century Mexico concerns the Church, an institution far more stable than the government and more accessible to historians than the military archives. For the 1830s and 1840s historians tend to shift to the North to explain the independence of Texas and the war with the United States. González Navarro's *Anatomía del poder* concerns the crucial but relatively stable interlude after the war with the United States and prior to the Revolution of Ayutla. By these devices historians have been able to pursue traditional research in the area of political instability. The results are the best work on the early nineteenth century. But archival research consistently leads us away from instability because of its methodological bias for order and stability. Studying the lulls in a period of instability avoids rather than explains the central problem. The rapid rotation of government personnel is not an annoying distraction or merely the prelude to civil war. It is the essential feature of instability in Latin America.[10]

In the end, Mexico's instability was transformed into civil war. After the mid-1850s Mexican politics were clearly polarized into opposing armies, thus clarifying their conflicts and facilitating historical research. Overt conflict between clearly defined opponents can be discussed using military analogies for strategic advantages, sources of support, and victory or defeat on the battlefield. Historians frequently have conjectured that the liberals were supported by some sort of middle stratum of the population, perhaps from the peripheral regions of Mexico, while the conservatives were supported by the old privileged classes usually resident in the national capital. This regional sociopolitical explanation has its roots in the military conflicts of the 1850s and 1860s, but the extension of this explanation back into the conflicts of the 1820s, 1830s, and 1840s has been problematic.

Richard Sinkin pioneered the quantitative approach to the study of nineteenth-century Mexican politics. His examination of the leaders of the mid-century Reform revealed the generational, occupational, and regional profile of the liberal leadership at mid-century, the issues that divided them, and their difficulties in stabilizing government and institutionalizing political power. Sinkin's work, and Peter Smith's analysis of the structure of politics in the twentieth century, demonstrated the utility of an explicitly quantitative approach to the study of Mexican politics, but little has been done in the last decade to build on this fundamental work.[11] Quantitative methods have specific advantages over traditional historical research and, when extended to a broader political spectrum over the first decades after independence, can provide a framework for an examination and reevaluation of the existing hypotheses concerning the nature and origins of Mexico's political instability.

This book attempts to analyze, quantify, and test the major explanations for Mexican instability proposed over the last several decades in the historical and qualitative social science literature. Most historians have chosen to use words to define and answer these questions, and, given the commonly accepted historical standards, qualitative historians can often avoid explicit discussion of methodology. The decisions about which subjects are important to study and which causes are likely to result in significant effects are usually implicit. No one intentionally begins to study the insignificant or the irrelevant, but conclusions may seem plausible and logical even when based on erroneous interpretations due to problems with sample size or the failure to systematically select cases. All conclusions require at least an implicit judgment as to size; for example, whether an effect is large or small, a thesis is important or trivial, a cause is fundamental or superficial. Similar controversies may revolve around what the sample size ought to be or whether an event is typical or exceptional. The advantage of explicit quantification is that all these questions have to be discussed openly. Quantification permits the testing of old speculations and the extraction of new insights from materials that are too large and seemingly amorphous to be handled by the ordinary, qualitative narrative approach. Each chapter in this book pursues the thread of one or another explanation through the existing literature, quantifying variables and testing relationships whenever possible. All have certain methodological considerations in common.

Both historians and political scientists have typically identified political instability in Latin America with the "palace revolution" and rapid turnover in the highest government positions. Some 229 men served as presidents or cabinet ministers in the decades following Mexico's independence. They form the core of this study. Political analysts have employed an operational definition of power that closely follows this focus on turnover in government offices. This definition attributes political power to those individuals who occupy formal positions in institutional hierarchies. Whether access to institutions provides power or whether power provides access to institutional position, the correlation between power and position is apparent. Positional analysis provides a simple technique for defining who has power, but it risks missing powerful people who have no formal position in the hierarchy. Such hidden powers may in fact exist, but the tendency in modern bureaucracies for power to be recognized in formal hierarchical position makes this phenomenon less likely to occur.[12] Positional analysis presents clear advantages to both analysis of decision-making and analysis of reputation in defining who has power, while the differences between these techniques in practice have proved to be small.[13]

Short-term explanations of instability frequently emphasize the primacy of economic and fiscal fluctuations. Theorists and historians have suggested that social stratification and political ideology were insignificant sources of conflict and that the roots of instability may be found in the fiscal crises that governments faced in the early republican years. Chapter 2 examines the relationship between annual variation in economic fluctuations, fiscal crises, and political instability.

The remaining chapters examine explanations of instability that begin from a different premise—that there was in all probability as much ideological consistency among Mexican politicians of this period as there would be among those of any nationality at any time. Chapter 3 examines the hypothesis that there was a thread of consistency in the struggles from the time of independence to the end of the Wars of the Reform and the French Intervention. Instability may be explained by the shifting alliances between militarists, conservatives, moderates, and radical liberals and their reliance on the army, the Church, militias, peasants, and urban crowds for political support. Some historians have suggested that these political conflicts were strongly influenced by the social and geographic origins and past experiences of their leaders. Chapter 4 examines explanations based on correlations between ideology and the occupations and careers of the political elite. Chapter 5 measures the effects of geographic origins, training, experience, and political positions on the durability of presidents and cabinet ministers. Chapter 6 reviews hypotheses that suggest a relationship between regional social structures and the origins of political factionalism. Chapter 7 takes a closer look at social stratification and the households of elite politicians resident in Mexico City.

Two

Accounting for

Caudillos

The prospect of independence promised benefits of increased domestic control of the economy and government to Mexicans with a variety of political and economic interests. But national sovereignty did not fulfill its promise. The Mexican economy faltered, and the violent struggles for control of the government lasted for half a century after independence. And, if the first half-century of independence was a complete disappointment in terms of economic growth and stable government, the next half-century was, at best, no more than a mixed blessing. The economy grew rapidly in the late nineteenth century, but the improvement was accompanied by imposed political stability and increasing social tensions which erupted in the Revolution of 1910. Clearly, the relationship between political stability (or lack thereof) and economic growth (or decline) is fundamental to understanding this period. Yet there is no consensus and little research on the source of the problem. As Robert Potash has noted, "The connection between fiscal difficulties and the political instability that characterized this period has long been assumed, but detailed historical studies of its fiscal philosophy, taxation administration, and deficit financing methods have been rare."[1]

One alternative is to blame the collapse of the Mexican economy after independence on the deleterious effect of political turmoil. John Coatsworth has argued that the two largest obstacles to economic growth in nineteenth-century Mexico were a national geography that made transportation relatively expensive and an inefficient legal structure which hindered the development of modern economic institutions. "The collapse of stable government," he writes, "nullified the potentially positive effects of the changes that accompanied independence and deprived both the new government and the private sector of the resources needed to improve transportation."[2] In other words, the fundamental problem was political; instability had fiscal and legal consequences (low income and failure to innovate) which not only prevented economic growth but led to its decline.

This explanation places the burden of causation in the political sphere, but analysis of political conflict in early republican Mexico has proved to be a formidable task. One traditional interpretation of instability discounts political motives. The proponents of this interpretation see politics as public expediency designed to disguise private ambitions. Politicians were unprincipled and idiosyncratic opportunists, called caudillos, who used "the then fashionable labels of liberalism and conservatism . . . to cover their personal rivalries."[3] The assumptions underlying this approach may be summarized as follows. Given the constraints of a rigid social structure, extremely unequal distribution of wealth, and narrowly limited economic opportunities, conquest of state power is an avenue of social mobility. The state occupies an intermediary role between the economically dominant class and the international order of states. By monopolizing this role, the caudillo and his band exploit state power for their own enrichment. Once having attained power, the caudillo must operate within narrow limits to avoid antagonizing groups whose power could be greater than his own, chiefly domestic landowners and foreign businessmen. Although industrialization, economic nationalism, or extensive land reform would be genuine threats to the social distribution of wealth and power, the change of government personnel itself is not. Hence, the opportunities for pillage are essentially static. Turnover is predictable and does not disrupt the social relations of power.[4]

If these are long-term, structural conditions, what explains short-term fluctuations in the rate of instability? Proponents of this interpretation contend that the availability of financial rewards determined the ability of caudillos to maintain their clients' loyalty. When a leader was unable to reward his followers, the alliance broke down and a new group replaced them in power. In the words of Wolf and Hansen, "The more limited the supply of ready wealth, the more rapid the turnover of caudillos."[5] This hypothesis echoes the complaints of contemporary observers that lower-level bureaucrats were chronically unemployed and willing to serve any government that promised to pay them regularly.[6] Justo Sierra, a nineteenth-century politician and historian, cited an aphorism from the period which said, "When salaries are paid, revolutions fade."[7]

Although examining the roots of economic change in the political system has proved difficult, the caudillo interpretation proposes that causation moves in the opposite direction. The hypothesis suggests that the peaks and troughs of economic cycles tossed caudillos into and out of office. The hypothesis that economic fluctuations determine instability has the advantage of simplifying historical reality in a way that facilitates the formulation of hypotheses and empirical tests; Sierra's rhyme can be evaluated quantitatively. By temporarily setting aside the complexity of political discourse as shadow rather than substance, this thesis precludes difficult judgments about the characteristics of rule, styles of altering the composition of governments, and the analysis of decision-making. Such a view has been expressed by both historians and political scientists who have typically identified political instability in Latin America with the "palace revolution" and rapid turnover in the highest government positions.

Whether called "an abrupt change of governmental personnel" or a "palace revolution," it is this frequent turnover in government positions which receives much of the attention when analysts write of political instability in Latin America. Historians often note that the Mexican presidency repeatedly changed hands in the decades after independence, but scholars have differed in their estimates of the degree of instability.[8] Clearly, much depends on how these changes are counted: whether interim presidents and temporary interim presidents should be included, whether to count discontinuous terms as multiple or single changes, and whether to exclude leaves of absence either for illness or to personally head the army during time of war or rebellion. In fact, attempts to draw qualitative distinctions between distinct rationales for political turnovers require judgments that are unavoidably impressionistic. How many resignations "for reasons of health" are really the result of covert political pressures?

Table 2.1 Number of Changes in National Executive Posts, 1825–1855

	President	War Minister	Finance Minister	Foreign Minister	Interior Minister	Total
1825	0	3	2	3	1	9
1826	0	0	0	1	0	1
1827	0	1	2	0	0	3
1828	0	3	2	1	1	7
1829	3	0	5	3	4	15
1830	1	1	1	1	1	5
1831	0	0	0	0	0	0
1832	2	2	1	3	4	12
1833	7	6	5	2	2	22
1834	1	3	6	0	2	12
1835	1	0	5	4	3	13
1836	1	1	3	0	1	6
1837	1	3	2	3	3	12
1838	0	4	3	3	7	17
1839	3	2	2	3	3	13
1840	0	0	0	1	5	6
1841	2	1	4	3	0	10
1842	1	0	0	0	1	2
1843	2	3	0	0	1	6
1844	4	5	4	4	1	18
1845	0	1	3	1	4	9
1846	4	6	16	7	9	42
1847	5	4	7	7	10	33
1848	2	3	6	2	3	16
1849	0	0	5	3	2	10
1850	0	0	4	0	0	4
1851	1	2	6	4	3	16
1852	0	2	1	5	3	11
1853	3	7	4	5	4	23
1854	0	3	4	0	0	7
1855	4	4	8	3	7	26

Sources: *Diccionario Porrúa de historia, biografía y geografía de México*, 5th ed., s.v. "Gobiernos de México"; *Enciclopedia de México*, s.v. "Gabinetes."

Figure 2.1   Total of Changes in National Executive Posts, 1825–1855

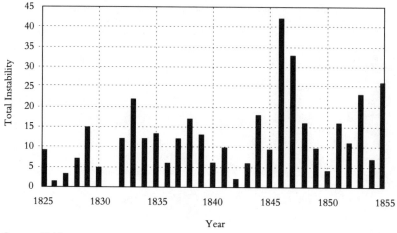

Source: Table 2.1.

A positional analysis has the advantage of avoiding potentially insoluble difficulties concerning the characteristics of rule, styles of altering the composition of governments, or the analysis of decision-making. Quantitative social scientists have found that cabinet insta-bility, resignations, dismissals, and the like consistently occurred during periods when the public showed dissatisfaction with the government.[9] This is consistent with the outline of nineteenth-century Mexican history. In early republican Mexico, cabinet insta-bility was endemic and accompanied by urban riots, demonstra-tions, assaults, and rural rebellions from independence to the Wars of the Reform and the French Intervention.[10]

When these alterations are counted without regard to their ap-parent or covert motives, the presidency changed hands forty-nine times during the first thirty-three years of republican government, from the initiation of constitutional government under the First Fed-eral Republic in October 1824 to the beginning of nearly ten years of civil war at the end of 1857.[11] Cabinet ministers entered and left office even more frequently. Annual sums of changes in Mexico's highest executive offices for each calendar year from the beginnings of the First Federal Republic to the triumph of the Revolution of Ayutla are presented in table 2.1. These totals of turnovers in the highest executive offices conform to qualitative impressions of "stability" and "instability."[12] There were only a few changes of executive personnel during the relatively calm years of 1826, 1827, 1831, and 1850. Much higher numbers in 1829, 1833/34, and during the War with the United States (1846 to 1848) and the Revolution of Ayutla (1854/55) reflect the increased turbulence of those years.

Table 2.2 Total National Government Income and Executive Instability, 1825–1844

	Total Income		Instability	
	$1,000s	Rank	Total	Rank
1825	15,455	4	6	7.5
1825/26	17,725	7	6	7.5
1826/27	17,017	5	3	4
1827/28	13,645	1	5	5
1828/29	14,593	3	11	13
1829/30	14,104	2	12	14
1830/31	18,392	8	0	1
1831/32	17,583	6	3	3
1832/33	20,563	9	22	19
1833/34	21,124	10	14	16
1834/35	n.a.		14	
1835/36	29,525	16	9	11
1836/37	21,822	12	8	10
1837/38	25,018	14	16	17
1839	29,137	15	13	15
1840	21,227	11	6	7.5
1841	23,996	13	10	12
1842	30,682	17	2	2
1843	34,139	19	6	7.5
1844	31,873	18	18	18

Statistics: Spearman's rho = 0.233. Kendall's tau = 0.111. Correlation coefficient = 0.206. r^2 = 0.042.
Notes: Total income figures for fiscal years 1825 (eight months), 1825/26 (ten months), and 1837/38 (eighteen months) were adjusted to twelve months to permit comparability with other fiscal years, all of which were twelve months in length. Income figures are thousands of Mexican pesos.
Sources: Tenenbaum, *The Politics of Penury*, pp. 178–179; *Diccionario Porrúa de historia, biografía y geografía de México*, 5th ed., s.v. "Gobiernos de México"; *Enciclopedia de México*, s.v. "Gabinetes."

Total turnovers in executive offices appear to be a good approximation of what has been called "political instability," but the accuracy of this and other measurements used here should not be overrated. Accordingly, testing of hypotheses will include annual rankings and other statistical tests which minimize the effect of random error.[13]

Table 2.2 tests the proposition that instability and low government income were closely related, but the data provide no support for this hypothesis. Of nineteen years included in the table, fewer than one-third conform to the suggested pattern: three years when income was high and instability low (1840, 1842, and 1843), and three years when low income coincided with high instability (1828/29, 1829/30, and 1832/33). More years contradict the expected pattern than conform to it; in seven different years high income coincided with high instability (1833/34 to 1839, 1841, 1844), and in six additional years governments were more stable despite relatively low income (1825 to 1827/28, 1830/31, and 1831/32). Although the hypothesis predicted a negative relationship, the results show a positive one. The relationship is weak and likely to result from chance alone.

At this level of generalization the hypothesis that instability and low government income were related might be rejected as unproved, but part of the problem may lie in the use of highly aggregated income figures which include funds from varied sources, most importantly tax revenues and loans. We would expect income from taxation and funds from government borrowing to have different relationships to instability. Faced with a deficit, raising loans was probably easier than increasing taxes.[14] Raising additional sums through taxation to cover the anticipated deficit was likely to increase social conflict and turmoil. Paradoxically, increased taxes would have required greater efficiency and strength from governments presumed to have been on the verge of collapse. Since it seems unlikely that a government could save itself from fiscal collapse by collecting more revenues, low tax collection would correlate with instability. Borrowing, on the other hand, probably offered a short-term solution to fiscal crisis.

Table 2.3 shows a positive correlation between years of instability and years of heavy government borrowing.[15] Instability remained at relatively low levels prior to 1832/33, and the sums bor-

Table 2.3   National Government Income from Foreign and
Domestic Loans and Executive Instability, 1825–1844

	Income from Loans		Instability	
	$1,000s	Rank	Total	Rank
1825	2,173	4	6	7.5
1825/26	2,981	7	6	7.5
1826/27	428	1	3	4
1827/28	813	2	5	5
1828/29	1,586	3	11	13
1829/30	2,380	6	12	14
1830/31	2,357	5	0	1
1831/32	3,735	9	3	3
1832/33	5,062	11	22	19
1833/34	4,240	10	14	16
1834/35	6,041	15	14	
1835/36	9,243	20	9	11
1836/37	5,530	13	8	10
1837/38	7,497	17	16	17
1839	7,728	18	13	15
1840	5,802	14	6	7.5
1841	5,151	12	10	12
1842	8,032	19	2	2
1843	3,090	8	6	7.5
1844	6,240	16	18	18

Statistics: Spearman's rho = 0.395. Kendall's tau = 0.263. Correlation coefficient = 0.364. $r^2 = 0.132$.
Notes: See table 2.2.
Sources: See table 2.2.

rowed by national governments during those years were relatively small. After the early 1830s, changes in top-level administrators were more frequent and governments borrowed larger sums of money, principally from domestic lenders. The correlation between instability and borrowing can be explained in two ways: in terms of changes in demand for loans or in terms of changes in their supply. Either creditors were more willing to loan money during periods of instability, or governments were more eager to borrow in unstable years. Only the second alternative makes sense. Since creditors would be expected to prefer loans to stable governments, instability

Table 2.4   Annual National Revenues from Taxation and
Executive Instability, 1825–1844

	Tax Revenues		Instability	
	$1,000s	Rank	Total	Rank
1825	11,406	11	6	7.5
1825/26	13,188	15	6	7.5
1826/27	12,300	14	3	4
1827/28	10,250	6	5	5
1828/29	10,927	9	11	13
1829/30	9,606	3	12	14
1830/31	13,202	16	0	1
1831/32	10,924	8	3	3
1832/33	9,587	4	22	19
1833/34	11,363	10	14	16
1834/35	n.a.		14	
1835/36	10,251	7	9	11
1836/37	7,074	1	8	10
1837/38	7,215	2	16	17
1839	10,000	5	13	15
1840	12,196	13	6	7.5
1841	11,807	12	10	12
1842	14,903	17	2	2
1843	17,027	19	6	7.5
1844	15,351	18	18	18

Statistics: Spearman's rho = −0.448. Kendall's tau = −0.346. Correlation coefficient = −0.332. r^2 = 0.110.
Notes: See table 2.2.
Sources: See table 2.2.

must have raised the interest rates charged when governments sought loans in unstable periods.

Instability coincided with revenue shortfalls. Table 2.4 shows a strong negative relationship between tax revenues and executive instability. Of a total of nineteen years for which data are available, almost 75 percent fit the expected pattern of high instability in years of low revenue collections, and greater stability in years when more taxes were collected.

Although these relationships are fairly strong, the direction of causation is more difficult to determine. The correlation between

instability and low revenue collections is ambiguous. Did governments borrow more money because instability prevented efficient
tax collections, or did economic cycles depress revenues causing
instability and forcing governments to turn to loans? Either hypothesis is consistent with the evidence at this level of generalization. Accepting both as true leads to the sort of circular argument
which might be mistaken for a complete explanation. In fact, such
an argument only obscures the fundamental relationship between
the economy, taxation, and politics in early nineteenth-century Mexico. To define this relationship more precisely, more explicit hypotheses must be examined.

A substantial case can be made for the argument that economic
fluctuations caused low revenue collections. Since the modern state
relies on taxation raised in money rather than in kind, taxes depend
on prices determined in markets; without well-functioning markets, abstract definitions of "value" are arbitrary and capricious.[16]
Economists and historians of fiscal systems point to the difficulties
of taxation in economies where markets and the use of currency are
insufficiently developed.[17] This problem in itself is likely to result
in considerable political conflict, the more so since those in the best
position to estimate any individual's wealth, that is, those closest to
him, are the most likely to be friends, enemies, or family, and
highly biased. In the words of Wolf and Hansen, "each hacendado's
bitterest enemy was potentially his closest neighbor."[18] In practice, Mexican governments found direct taxes extremely difficult
to collect.[19]

In such economies the foreign trade sector is frequently the
most commercialized. Harley H. Hindricks noted the importance
of foreign trade in determining the size of government revenue's
share of the national product in modern low-income countries.
"Openness," which he defined as the ratio of imports to national
income, was most significant in countries where per capita income
was below $150, since in such cases the market and use of currency
were largely limited to foreign trade and associated transactions.[20]
Merle Kling suggested a direct relationship between foreign trade
taxes and caudillo politics. "The larger the percentage of government revenues derived from the 'external' sector, the more nearly
does political behavior conform to the configuration of the type of
politics characterized as *caudillismo*."[21] In his study of the relation-

ship between Latin American political systems and dependence on foreign trade since World War II, Kling found a significant correlation between caudillo politics and "a tax structure which relies heavily on the 'external' sector as a source of revenue."[22] All of the states Kling regarded as conforming to the caudillo model obtained more than 30 percent of government revenues from foreign trade.[23] Barbara Tenenbaum has made a similar argument for nineteenth-century Mexico, concluding that taxes on international trade led to revolts:

> Like many other republics in similar circumstances, [Mexico] based its new fiscal system on taxes to be levied on international trade. Unfortunately, customs duties never produced enough revenue to pay for the ordinary expenses of government, leaving politicians in power unable to reward supporters and buy off opponents. Revolts inevitably ensued as ambitious officers struggled to control the few resources available, and other nations invaded hoping to capitalize on Mexican weakness.[24]

Taxation of foreign trade presents two major problems which increase the likelihood of conflict and instability: supervision of collections and international trade fluctuations. First, given the high cost of transportation in nineteenth-century Mexico, the ports and border crossings were relatively far from the capital and other centers of population. If high costs of supervising the collection of foreign trade taxes allowed customs officials to pilfer from the treasury, the national government's dependence on trade taxes collected in the periphery threatened the government's fiscal basis. The national government's main source of income was highly vulnerable to dissident caudillos who found it easy to appropriate customs revenues to pay their own armies. Second, dependence on taxation of foreign trade meant that revenues were subject to the vicissitudes of economic fluctuations as well. If total revenues largely depend on international trade fluctuations and business cycles, a decline in foreign trade will lead to government revenue shortfalls.[25] This fact did not go unnoticed by Mexican treasury ministers. In 1841 Ignacio Trigueros noted the difference between the old colonial system of internal taxes and the republican tax system which depended largely on foreign commerce, saying, "if foreign commerce is disabled for any reason, the nation is left in penury."[26]

Table 2.5   Annual Revenues from Foreign Trade Taxes, 1825–1844

	Foreign Trade Revenues	
	$1,000s	% of Total
1825	4,594	60.42
1825/26	6,571	59.79
1826/27	8,049	65.44
1827/28	5,912	57.68
1828/29	6,684	61.17
1829/30	4,987	51.92
1830/31	8,483	64.26
1831/32	7,550	69.11
1832/33	7,764	75.54
1833/34	9,052	80.54
1834/35	9,241	n.a.
1835/36	6,200	60.48
1836/37	4,738	66.98
1837/38	5,357	75.73
1839	5,578	55.78
1840	8,310	68.14
1841	6,598	55.88
1842	6,034	40.49
1843	8,507	49.96
1844	8,254	53.77

Notes: The category "Foreign Trade Revenues" includes *importación, toneladas, internación,* and *esportación.* Percentages were based on the total of revenues from foreign and domestic trade taxation, monopolies and state enterprises, and sale of national property. Loans, deposits, and balances were excluded from the total for each year. All fiscal years were twelve months in length except for 1825 (eight months), 1825/26 (ten months), and 1837/38 (eighteen months). Revenue figures are thousands of Mexican pesos.
Sources: Miguel Lerdo de Tejada, *Comercio esterior de México* (Mexico: Impreso por R. Rafael, 1853), table 36; México, Secretaría de Hacienda, *Memoría,* 1825–1844.

In a provocative study, Warren Dean provided empirical evidence of links between foreign commerce and political instability. Dean found that a five-year moving average of the total number of illegal and unscheduled changes of heads of state in Latin American countries was inversely correlated with the value of imports of all Latin American countries from Great Britain and the United States. When trade declined, more governments were overthrown. Although

Table 2.6   British, French, and United States Exports
to Mexico, 1825–1851

	Exports to Mexico (1,000s of Mexican Pesos)			
	British	French	United States	Total
1825	n.a.	3,680	n.a.	n.a.
1826	n.a.	2,860	6,281	n.a.
1827	3,464	2,985	4,173	10,622
1828	1,535	1,998	2,886	6,419
1829	1,518	1,947	2,331	5,796
1830	4,892	4,645	4,837	14,374
1831	3,644	4,071	6,178	13,893
1832	999	2,680	3,468	7,147
1833	2,107	3,005	5,408	10,520
1834	2,298	2,408	5,265	9,971
1835	2,014	3,460	9,029	14,503
1836	1,274	1,900	6,041	9,215
1837	2,601	1,928	3,880	8,409
1838	2,199	1,635	2,787	6,621
1839	3,301	2,268	2,164	7,733
1840	2,327	2,799	2,515	7,641
1841	2,175	2,531	2,037	6,743
1842	1,875	2,281	1,535	5,691
1843	2,990	2,389	1,472	6,851
1844	2,470	2,765	1,795	7,030
1845	2,736	2,540	1,159	6,435
1846	1,518	2,079	1,531	5,128
1847	503	680	238	1,421
1848	4,730	n.a.	4,054	n.a.
1849	3,895	n.a.	9,091	n.a.
1850	n.a.	n.a.	2,013	n.a.
1851	n.a.	n.a.	1,582	n.a.

Sources: French and U.S. exports to Mexico are from Miguel Lerdo de Tejada, *Comercio esterior de México* (Mexico: Impreso por R. Rafael, 1853), tables 38 and 41. Following Robert A. Potash, "El 'Comercio Esterior de México' de Miguel Lerdo de Tejada: Un Error Estadístico," *Trimestre Económico* 20 (1953): 474–479, I have used British export figures from G. R. Porter, *The Progress of the Nation, in Various Social and Economic Relations, from the Beginning of the Nineteenth Century,* 3d ed. (London: John Murray, 1851), pp. 362–367.

this work is suggestive, the high degree of aggregation involved leaves the direction and strength of casual relationships open to question.[27]

Mexico in the early nineteenth century seems to fit into the patterns proposed by these hypotheses. Mexican per capita income was below $150 (in U.S. dollars of 1950 value) for the entire nineteenth century.[28] Taxes on the "external" sector amounted on average to about 60 percent of government revenues from 1825 to 1844 and varied from a minimum of 40 percent in 1842 to as much as 80 percent in 1833/34 (table 2.5). Moreover, fluctuations in Mexico's foreign trade were rapid and extreme; total Mexican imports from Great Britain, France, and the United States varied from over 14 million pesos in 1830, 1831, and 1835 to less than half that amount in 1828, 1829, and 1838 (table 2.6).[29] Such fluctuations in foreign

Table 2.7 Foreign Trade and Executive Instability, 1827–1844

	Foreign Trade		Instability	
	$1,000s	Rank	Total	Rank
1827	10,622	15	3	3
1828	6,419	3	7	8
1829	5,796	2	16	15.5
1830	14,375	17	5	4
1831	13,893	16	0	1
1832	7,147	8	12	12
1833	10,520	14	22	18
1834	9,971	13	10	9.5
1835	14,503	18	13	13.5
1836	9,215	12	6	6
1837	8,409	11	11	11
1838	6,621	4	16	15.5
1839	7,733	10	13	13.5
1840	7,641	9	6	6
1841	6,743	5	10	9.5
1842	5,691	1	2	2
1843	6,851	6	6	6
1844	7,030	7	18	17

Statistics: Spearman's rho = −0.160. Kendall's tau = −0.127. Correlation coefficient = −0.216. r^2 = 0.047.
Sources: See tables 2.1 and 2.6.

trade and associated revenues would seem to promise support for the general hypothesis that economic cycles caused instability.

Annual amounts of foreign trade and instability are compared in table 2.7. Of the eighteen years from 1827 through 1844, only half conform to the pattern suggested by the hypothesis; five were years of relatively low trade and high instability; and in four years trade was high and instability low. An equal number of years contradict the expected pattern: five years when low instability corresponded with low foreign trade, and four years when high instability coincided with a high value of such trade value. These results show only random variation; there is no evidence of a strong relationship between cycles in foreign trade and instability.[30]

It might be argued that total import value is not the best variable to use in testing this hypothesis. Many observers noted the persistence of contraband trade and the limited ability of Mexican governments to collect foreign trade taxes. Since the figures used in the previous tables were based on the value of exports to Mexico from Britain, France, and the United States as they were measured by officials of those countries rather than Mexican customs officers and statisticians, these figures may include most of Mexico's contraband as well as its legal imports.[31] Thus, the figures may not discriminate between the effects of trade cycles and variation in the efficiency of collections. The amount of contraband trade would increase during periods of poor supervision of collections and periods of instability. If so, foreign trade (including a large proportion of contraband) might be relatively high, while at the same time revenue collections were low. This hypothesis involves a circular argument: trade revenues decline because instability reduces the efficiency of revenue collections, allowing more contraband, which results in lower government revenues, which in turn causes more instability when salaries cannot be paid. Although the hypothesis is not clear about where the chain of events begins and which links are more important, it suggests that instability is more closely related to revenues derived from foreign trade than to the value of foreign trade itself. Table 2.8 compares data and annual rankings of total foreign trade taxation with figures on executive instability, but the statistics show little association between them. Circular reasoning and weak quantitative evidence do nothing to support this hypothesis.

Table 2.8 Foreign Trade Taxes and Executive Instability, 1825–1844

	Foreign Trade Taxes		Instability	
	$1,000s	Rank	Total	Rank
1825	6,890	10	6	7.5
1825/26	7,886	13	6	7.5
1826/27	8,049	14	3	4
1827/28	5,912	5	5	5
1828/29	6,684	9	11	13
1829/30	4,987	3	12	14
1830/31	8,483	17	0	1
1831/32	7,550	11	3	3
1832/33	7,764	12	22	20
1833/34	9,052	19	14	16.5
1834/35	9,241	20	14	16.5
1835/36	6,200	7	9	11
1836/37	4,738	2	8	10
1837/38	3,571	1	16	18
1839	5,578	4	13	15
1840	8,310	16	6	7.5
1841	6,598	8	10	12
1842	6,034	6	2	2
1843	8,057	18	6	7.5
1844	8,254	15	18	19

Statistics: Spearman's rho = -0.049. Kendall's tau = -0.064. Correlation coefficient = -0.078. $r^2 = 0.006$.
Sources: See tables 2.1 and 2.5.

To clarify the situation, another link in this chain of events connecting low trade revenues with executive instability may be tested. Suppose the rate of tariff collection to vary with the stability of the government and its success at limiting contraband. For example, if an unstable government were unable to enforce revenue collections, large amounts of contraband slipping past customs collectors would produce a ratio of Mexico's foreign trade tax revenues that was very low in relation to the value of that trade; a low tax-trade ratio would correspond to more unstable government. Tariff collection rates ought to have been lower in unstable years and higher when there were fewer changes in top government positions.

Table 2.9   Tax/Trade Ratio and Executive Instability, 1827–1844

	Tax/Trade		Instability	
	Ratio	Rank	Total	Rank
1827	0.657	7	3	3
1828	0.981	12	7	8
1829	1.007	13	16	15.5
1830	0.469	1	5	4
1831	0.577	5	0	1
1832	1.071	15	12	12
1833	0.799	9	22	18
1834	0.917	10	10	9.5
1835	0.532	3	13	13.5
1836	0.593	6	6	6
1837	0.494	2	11	11
1838	0.539	4	16	15.5
1839	0.721	8	13	13.5
1840	1.088	16	6	6
1841	0.978	11	10	9.5
1842	1.060	14	2	2
1843	1.242	18	6	6
1844	1.174	17	18	18

Statistics: Spearman's rho = 0.070. Kendall's tau = 0.047. Correlation coefficient = 0.082. $r^2 = 0.007$.
Sources: See tables 2.1, 2.5, and 2.6.

The evidence in table 2.9 does not support this hypothesis. There is no systematic relationship between the rate of tariff collections on foreign trade and executive instability. As large a number of cases contradict the hypothesis as conform to it, and the measures of association are weak. The distribution of ranks is that to be expected by random variation alone. Instability was not correlated with the tariff collection rate; low levels of foreign trade taxation do not indicate that inefficient collections and contraband undermined the fiscal foundations of the state. Governments that successfully extracted a higher proportion of foreign trade in taxes were as likely to be unstable as governments which took a smaller percentage. Mexico's foreign trade was highly variable, but fluctuations in that trade appear to be unrelated to turnover rates among presidents and cabinet ministers.

If rapid and extreme fluctuations in foreign trade did not cause instability, why did foreign trade vary so dramatically? The ratio of tariff collections to foreign trade is one measure of the degree of protection afforded to Mexican producers against their foreign competitors. Robert Potash has described the attempts by some radicals to restrict foreign trade in the interests of domestic artisans, while some conservatives sought protection to aid a nascent group of industrialists.[32] The rate of tariff collections was highly restrictive under Vicente Guerrero, Valentín Gómez Farías, and Antonio López de Santa Anna in 1829, 1832, 1834, 1840, and from 1842 to 1844. Collection rates were much lower in 1827, 1830, and from 1835 to 1838. Tariff collection rates and the total value of British, French, and U.S. exports to Mexico are compared in table 2.10. The correspondence between the two series is striking. During the years when

Table 2.10   Tax/Trade Ratio and Foreign Trade, 1827–1844

| | Tax/Trade | | Foreign Imports | |
	Ratio	Rank	Total	Rank
1827	0.657	7	10,622	15
1828	0.981	12	6,419	3
1829	1.007	13	5,796	2
1830	0.469	1	14,375	17
1831	0.577	5	13,893	16
1832	1.071	15	7,147	8
1833	0.799	9	10,520	14
1834	0.917	10	9,971	13
1835	0.532	3	14,503	18
1836	0.593	6	9,215	12
1837	0.494	2	8,409	11
1838	0.539	4	6,621	4
1839	0.721	8	7,733	10
1840	1.088	16	7,641	9
1841	0.978	11	6,743	5
1842	1.060	14	5,691	1
1843	1.242	18	6,851	6
1844	1.174	17	7,030	7

Statistics: Spearman's rho = -0.620. Kendall's tau = -0.477. Correlation coefficient = -0.669. $r^2 = 0.448$.
Sources: See tables 2.5 and 2.6.

the tariff/trade ratios were lower, Mexico's trading partners exported more to Mexico. When a greater percentage of the trade was taken in taxes, Britain, France, and the United States exported less to Mexico. Of eighteen years included in the table, sixteen conform to the expected pattern. During one of the two exceptions, 1838, the French blockaded Veracruz, limiting imports more than the tariffs alone would have done. All three measures of association are decidedly negative. These results are evidence that fluctuations in foreign trade resulted from political decisions. Taken together, these results support the thesis that annual economic variations are not as important as the root causes of instability as are continuing political disputes.

Comparison of economic, fiscal, and political variations in early republican Mexico indicates that political changes caused economic fluctuations rather than the reverse. Political instability was not correlated with the national government's total income since loans and foreign trade taxes, the two major components of total income, were inversely related. Political instability was positively correlated with borrowing but negatively correlated with revenue from taxation. These correlations suggest that when political instability reduced revenues from taxation, governments sought loans to make up for the revenue shortfalls. Plausible hypotheses and other studies have suggested that international economic fluctuations create fiscal crises which determine the rate of instability. Taxes on foreign trade provided the largest proportion of national government revenue. On average, 60 percent, and, at times, as high as 80 percent of national government revenues came from taxes on foreign trade. The value of this foreign trade fluctuated widely, but cyclical depressions did not cause instability either. Historians and political scientists have assumed that caudillos were rapacious, unprincipled leaders who were tossed into and out of office by the peaks and troughs of economic cycles, but evidence indicates that Mexico's political leaders themselves determined the level of foreign trade rather than merely suffering from trade cycles. Turnover rates in the highest government offices were not determined by the value of foreign trade or by the amounts the national government received from taxation of that trade. Lack of correlation between instability and the tariff collection rate on foreign trade suggests that contraband, incompetence, and corruption were not significant causes of instability either. On the contrary, Mexico's foreign trade varied as the result of political decisions made by Mexico's leaders. Variations in trade levels were correlated with the relative rate of taxation on foreign trade. Fluctuating tariffs created oscillations in foreign trade; political decisions set off economic and fiscal vibrations.

The apolitical caudillo has played a useful role in cutting through the complexity of political conflict of this period and encouraging the formulation of hypotheses to explain instability, fiscal constraints, and economic fluctuations. But the caudillo model of the relationship between the economy and political conflict in Mexico is not consistent with the available historical data. Economic fluctuations did not change the rate of instability. Since politicians did not merely respond to economic cycles but caused them, the apolitical caudillo has no further role to play in explaining the nexus of politics and economics in this period of Mexican history. The time has come to move beyond the myth which blames the crisis of early republican Mexico on the personalities of politicians, economic crises, and short-term fiscal fluctuations. Instability requires an explanation that takes political differences seriously.

Three

Political Conflict in Early

Republican Mexico

The argument that Mexican politicians in this period were unusually unprincipled and inconsistent is based on isolated anecdotes and generalizations from a few examples rather than on systematic study. The assumption that political positions were volatile and superficial, whether true or not, has tended to fragment, even atomize, the study of Mexican politics. Although such suggestions can be spun into theories of instability, the working hypothesis that political discourse was only a cloak for ambitious and idiosyncratic individuals fails to cover the conflicts or explain the instability that followed independence. This chapter and those that follow begin from a different premise, that is, that there was in all probability as much consistency of principle among early nineteenth-century Mexican politicians as there was among those of any other nationality at any other time.

Many volumes on Mexican politics, from the nineteenth-century histories of José María Luis Mora and Lucas Alamán to current textbooks, describe a sharp dichotomy between liberals and conservatives. David Brading has suggested that this "crude dichotomy" reflects the tendency of historians during the nineteenth century to portray conflicts in dualistic terms. Where liberals saw "a conflict between the forces of progress and reaction," conservatives described "a struggle between anarchy and civilization."[1] Modern authors may have succumbed to what Josefina Vázquez has called "the liberal tradition of superimposing the goals of the liberals and conservatives of the era of the Reforma onto the as yet undefined struggles" of the years before 1846.[2] There were no political parties in early republican Mexico in the sense that we would use the term today, but there is abundant argument in the literature that distinct factions did exist from the 1820s to the 1860s. This chapter will spell out the case for a working hypothesis that Mexican politics between 1821 and 1867 was visibly fragmented into conservative, moderate, and radical factions. The general thesis sketched here will lead to specific testable hypotheses which will be examined and evaluated over the remainder of the book.

For Mexican conservatives the ideal state would regulate social and economic life through an elaborate civil bureaucracy, a strong military, and the moral monopoly of the Catholic Church. Conservatives favored explicit social control designed to preserve class differences and social hierarchy. Conservatives sought a society resistant to social and economic mobility, a society based on the acceptance of social inequality, one in which authority and tradition were respected. Conservatives identified that tradition with the Catholic Church and an ordered social structure. The Church was to exercise social control indirectly through its monopoly of education and dominion over birth, death, and marriage rituals and records. The close relations between the Church hierarchy and the upper classes and the extensive wealth of the Church insured its political influence and economic power. Mexican conservatism was based on "the religious principle, the principle of property, the principle of family, the principle of morality."[3]

Mexican liberals held familiar positions in support of constitutionalism, freedom of the press, freedom of association, and juridical equality, but divided among themselves on the value of the Spanish past, republicanism, secularization, and the condition of the lower classes.[4] Those who were more moderate saw some good in the colonial past. The reforms of the Spanish enlightenment showed moderates the possibilities of enlightened, liberal monarchy. Of course, not all liberals were so sanguine about the colonial heritage. Lorenzo de Zavala, a notorious radical, saw no precedents for reform in the Spanish tradition and dismissed the colonial period as the reign of "terror and ignorance."[5] Radicals preferred a republic to constitutional monarchy, but moderates were less inclined to identify liberalism with republicanism. When Fernando VII refused the crown of Mexico and Iturbide's empire collapsed, moderates reluctantly accepted the republic, while radicals regarded republicanism as a requirement for social improvement.[6] Later, when conservatives and monarchists brought a Hapsburg archduke to Mexico to restore monarchy in the 1860s, moderates such as Pedro Escudero y Echánove and José Fernando Ramírez found Maximilian's liberal constitutionalism to their liking and served in his cabinet. Radicals, like Benito Juárez, remained insistent that only a republic could guarantee liberty and sovereignty.

Moderates were united in principle with radical liberals on the idea of reducing the political and economic power of the clergy, but moderates were less insistent on immediate action. Most moderates hoped to retain the traditional alliance between Church and state to one degree or another. Moderates rejected Valentín Gómez Farías's radical reforms of 1833–1834 and his later attempts to mortgage and sell Church property to save the government when Mexico was invaded by the United States. Moderates, of course, made this argument on appropriately liberal grounds, that the expropriation of the Church was an assault on the most sacred principle of liberalism, the right to property. Such attacks, they argued, must inevitably lead to the end of political liberty. Moderates, conservatives, and the Church supported a rebellion by certain militia units and forced the government to withdraw the 1847 decree.[7] Later, in the Constitutional Convention of 1856/57, moderates defeated a motion to allow explicit religious toleration and to separate the Church and state.

The issue of state power and its relation to the social hierarchy divided conservatives from moderates and moderates from radicals. Conservatives favored a bureaucratic, interventionist state. This emphasis on a strong state and established institutions required that political power be exercised by government institutions rather than through direct class rule. The conservative state was stronger and potentially more autonomous than the state favored by moderates. Moderates wanted a weaker state which required less taxation and allowed greater exercise of private economic power. As a method of social control, moderate liberalism sought the indirect exercise of power through legal guarantees of contracts and property rights, and the moral suasion of family, public schools, and a disestablished church. Moderate liberalism appears politically more open, competitive, and flexible at the same time that social control and political power are more directly held by an economic elite.

Radical liberals, in contrast, found that the struggle to disestablish the Church required, in the words of Charles Hale, "the solidification of state power to combat clerical privilege."[8] The struggle against entrenched wealth, privilege, and power demanded an increasingly powerful state, more taxes and expropriations, and larger armies to fight for equality. Ironically, in attempting to limit the use of the state to support wealth and inequality, the radicals themselves built an increasingly powerful state apparatus. Moderates could afford to assume equality; for them, liberalism was a method, an end in itself. For radicals, liberty and equality were goals they would attain only through the use of state power, power that could produce economically efficient results even at the cost of liberal political practice.[9]

Conservatives upheld the rights of traditional corporations and rejected liberal innovations. They regarded liberal notions of freedom as foreign, feared that civil rights and religious toleration would lead to anarchy, and identified republicanism with the mob rule of the French Revolution. Democracy was a foreign doctrine without roots in the Spanish or Aztec past. Federalism they regarded as a "disorganizing doctrine," and they argued that Mexico's heterogeneity required centralization.[10] Lucas Alamán called federalism "the most powerful and destructive devise imaginable."[11]

Alamán argued that the independence promised by federalism was illusory. In reality, federalism promised enslavement to foreign commerce which he called "the most miserable dependence that can be imagined."[12] Conservatives could no longer rely on merchants to support them. Independence destroyed the influence of the *consulados*, and contraband trade evaded monopoly interests. Commerce was still controlled by foreigners, although the foreigners were now British and French rather than Spanish. Foreign power behind the alliance of Mexican wholesale merchants and their foreign counterparts gave these merchants special privileges in Mexico and allowed them to absorb the public treasury through usury while blocking income to the treasury and the development of industry through contraband trade.[13] Conservative economic philosophy was pragmatic and included a willingness to use the apparatus and resources of the state to promote and protect wealth. They supported centralization of government power and strong state intervention to direct the economy rather than liberal laissez-faire.[14] Conservative regimes were often economically progressive and engaged in public construction and development projects.

Moderate liberals opposed monopoly and rejected state manipulation of the economy. Moderates were more likely to favor laissez-faire and were generally tolerant of foreign capital. Even many radicals such as Lorenzo de Zavala and Miguel Lerdo de Tejada believed that some competition was necessary for development. They favored "prudent" taxes on foreign imports to benefit merchants and consumers rather than high protective tariffs to favor industry. Radicals opposed regressive interior customs and monopolies while proposing direct and progressive taxation of income. They believed that an active interventionist state should promote economic development.[15] Other radicals, such as Vicente Guerrero, sought to use state power to exclude imported goods that competed with the products of domestic artisans, to exclude foreign merchants from retail sales, and to expel Spanish-born residents of Mexico.[16]

The conservative alliance of Church and army suffered major structural weaknesses. The Catholic Church emerged from the independence wars weakened but hopeful. Still the richest single corporation in Mexico,[17] the Church hoped the new nation would turn its back on the liberalizing reforms of the late eighteenth century and restore the Church to its traditional place as a pillar of the state at least equal in strength to the civil bureaucracy. In fact, independence seemed to promise the Church greater freedom from civil authority than had ever been enjoyed during the colonial period. Arguing that the *patronato real* had been granted solely to the Spanish monarchs who no longer ruled Mexico and not the republican governments that followed independence, the Church claimed that independence for Mexico granted the Church independence from interference by civil authorities.[18]

The claim to greater autonomy and strength was made by a correspondingly desperate and weakened Church hierarchy. During the independence wars bishops had not been appointed, while positions were vacated through death, emigration, and exile. Seminaries closed and fewer new priests were trained, while the absence of episcopates left the lower clergy free of supervision, aggravating the social division of the clergy. The Spanish crown refused to recognize the independence of Mexico and continued to claim not only civil authority but the right to exercise the patronato real as well. The king refused to name new bishops and blocked nominations from Rome as the stalemate continued. By 1829 Mexico did not have a single bishop.[19]

The Church's pretension to greater freedom from government interference left it increasingly weakened economically as well. Independence seemed to promise the end of the drain of wealth from Church to king and state, but the Church could not escape the general trends of the Mexican economy. The postwar depression reduced the value of clerical investments, while ecclesiastical contributions and taxes were subject to changes in law which recognized what taxpayers' refusal to pay had already accomplished, in fact, the abolition of the tithe.[20] The ostentation of the Church continued to give the impression of wealth and power while Church income declined due to late payments, frequent loss of capital, and the general depression of the national economy. Clerical investment policies exaggerated these effects and contributed to depressed income. Most loans were made at traditional, fixed interest on mortgages secured by real estate. No attempt was made to make more productive investments; in fact, no attempt was made to determine for what purpose a loan would be used.[21] The potential of Church resources to direct and promote social savings and economic growth was not realized.

Although conservatives proposed to base government on traditional corporate privileges, the Church was greatly weakened by independence, while the army was opportunistic and, at least initially, held no allegiance to general conservative principles. Like the Church, the Mexican military emerged from the independence wars with the promise of a greater place in the new state. During most of Mexico's three hundred years under the Spanish crown, military forces had been small and subservient to civil authority. These traditions were weakened when the financial desperation of Bourbon monarchs in the late eighteenth century, combined with the need to defend the colony against foreign aggression, encouraged a melding of local interest with military power in the militias.[22] After independence, much of the small royalist army had been shipped back to Spain, and few insurgent leaders survived the wars. Most of the officers were former royalists who had defended the crown in the creole militias and Spanish army.

Conservatives relied on the national army and planned to abolish the provincial and civic militias. Radicals, in contrast, depended on the civic and provincial militias and hoped to use them to replace the national army. Moderates were characteristically equivocal. They supported the idea of arming property-owning citizens in support of the government as a lower cost alternative to the professional army, but many moderates complained that civic militias were often filled with the worse social elements who would rather attack property than protect it. They complained that the national army drained the national treasury and tyrannized the country instead of defending it. Finding neither force entirely satisfactory, moderates hoped to restrict the power and privileges of the national army while limiting the militia units to those controlled by the propertied classes.[23]

The social composition of the militia varied over time and between units. Richard Packenham, the British consul in Mexico in 1833, reported that the civic militia of Mexico City was "a force composed of the very dregs of the people, without discipline or subordination, and ready to take advantage of any opportunity to plunder and commit excesses."[24] Arrangoiz supports this judgment, calling the militia a "vulgar rabble."[25] While militia units were supposed to be composed entirely of unpaid volunteers, radicals seemed to have paid them at least part of the time. Valentín Gómez Farías allegedly controlled the Sixth Battalion in 1833 and provided the men with three meals a day. Later, his son led the "Libertad" Battalion which was paid by the national government. Shaw suggests that these battalions served as Gómez Farías's private army.[26] Some militia units in 1847 included artisans, employees, and tobacco workers, but Prieto noted that the "Victoria" Battalion was composed of a majority of merchants and included doctors, legislators, and hacendados. He described their captain, Don Pedro Torrín, as a "misanthropic capitalist, as rigid as an iron bar and as retrograde as knee breeches."[27] Not surprisingly, the "Victoria" Battalion rebelled in favor of the Church in 1847.

Conservative allegiance to the Church and reliance on a paid professional army forced an uneasy, and in some ways, contradictory alliance between the cross and the sword. This contradiction is most clearly evident in the behavior of Antonio López de Santa Anna. In many ways Santa Anna was beyond even conservatism in his extravagant attempts to increase state power. Santa Anna attempted to build a strong state led by a powerful executive, and he refused to let elections or democratic-republican ideology interfere with his plans. When congresses objected to his extraordinary powers, he sent troops to disperse them, preferring legislative bodies which he chose himself. Santa Anna required a strong army and defended the authority of military tribunals against the radical assault of 1833. He revived special courts for merchants and miners that had been abolished at independence. He tried to increase funds for the government by any means possible; when the wealthy resisted further taxation and enforced loans in 1843, Santa Anna sent government agents to enter their homes and confiscate pianos and expensive furniture.[28]

Santa Anna might seem conservative in his support of the army and distaste for liberalism and representative democracy, but he regarded the Church as a threat to the power of the centralized state and as a potential source of income for the government. Santa Anna allowed radicals to plan the elimination of ecclesiastical property under his auspices. When Gómez Farías and other liberals attempted to weaken the Church in 1833, Santa Anna supported them until the radicals threatened the power of the army as well.[29] During the war with the United States, Santa Anna again supported Gómez Farías's plans to sell ecclesiastical property but accepted a "loan" of $100,000 from the Church when militia units and moderates rebelled against the plan.[30] Santa Anna's motives were apparently fiscal rather than ideological; his own assaults on Church property were insistent but limited actions designed to secure funds and weaken the Church without alienating his conservative allies. Santa Anna repeatedly confiscated Church property as he attempted to set up a powerful centralized state in the early 1840s. He abolished the Colegio Mayor de Santos and confiscated its endowment. He sold property belonging to Dominican and Mercedarian friars and put the Fonda Piadoso de Californias directly under the army's control. When the Archicofradía del Rosario refused to turn over $20,000 destined to support the hospital of San Juan de Dios, he sent troops to take the money by force.[31] Significantly, Lucas Alamán found it necessary to scold Santa Anna, pointing out that the Catholic

Church was "the only common link which binds all Mexicans, when all the rest have been broken."[32]

In a nineteenth-century republic as diverse as Mexico, eligibility to participate in elections was a fundamental indication of the underlying social support for political factions. In the elections of 1812, most males were enfranchised without literacy or property qualifications,[33] but after independence moderates and conservatives pressed to restrict suffrage. Even José María Luis Mora, an ally of Valentín Gómez Farías, argued in classic liberal fashion that only property owners ought to vote.[34] The conservative Lucas Alamán was a more vocal critic of the representative system, saying that in Mexico "the representative system is no mere fiction, as it is almost everywhere else, but a true irony."[35] Conservatives preferred a more restricted electorate; when they increased restrictions on suffrage in 1836, they effectively excluded 60 percent of the previously eligible voters.[36]

Valentín Gómez Farías, in contrast, appealed directly to the urban masses and called the people "the most valuable part of our society."[37] With other radicals he sought a society in which "the people, or, that is, the majority of the nation, would be the source from which all power emanates."[38] Conservatives and most moderates argued that Gómez Farías's concept of democracy was nothing more than an excuse for demagoguery. They referred to the lower class as "el populacho," "los léperos," or "la chusma," a sort of criminal underclass which they distinguished from honest workers. The distinction seems to have been more a political prejudice than a sociological fact; Shaw has argued that the classification is imprecise and that arrest records reveal "a cross-section of the laboring poor driven to crime and vagrancy by underemployment and unemployment."[39]

With the exception of the sack of the Parián in 1828, the activities of the urban masses have received little attention from modern historians, but evidence exists that some radicals were willing to take advantage of mass dissatisfaction to force changes in government personnel and policies. Lorenzo de Zavala estimated that as many as 30,000 or 40,000 people aided the civic militia in the Acordada Revolt in support of Vicente Guerrero in 1828. When the crowd looted the exclusive shops of the Parián market after the victory, Zavala and others regretted their part in the revolt since it had led to disorder and the destruction of property. But not all radicals turned from mass support. Valentín Gómez Farías relied on the civic militia and called out all citizens between the ages of eighteen and fifty to support his radical reforms after his residence was attacked by conservative troops in 1833. Urban crowds could create instability among the national executive elite. In 1838, a mob invaded the galleries of the Chamber of Deputies, forcing the resignation of unpopular ministers and winning the release from prison of Gómez Farías and José María Alpuche. Through his influence with people in the neighborhood of his prison cell, General José de Urrea was able to direct a conspiracy, escape his imprisonment, and lead a surprise attack on the national palace in 1840. There he was joined by Gómez Farías, who once again "called on the people to take arms." That attempt failed, but four years later an urban mob, armed civilian militia, and portions of the regular army combined to end the presidency of Santa Anna in what Guillermo Prieto called "a paragon of the popular revolution."[40]

Radicals had a long history of appeals to "the rabble," but moderates and conservatives seldom sought armed popular support. The few apparent exceptions are on a much smaller scale as well. In 1840 the priest of the parish of San Miguel in Mexico City organized his flock and threatened a riot if new elections were not held to reverse the results of what he alleged was vote fraud by the liberals.[41] Priests and monks took to the streets in December 1846 to protest Gómez Farías's plan to expropriate Church property, but the riots which occurred the following day were weak and uncoordinated. Order was quickly restored; it was the revolt by conservative and moderate militias, not mob action, that forced the government to withdraw the decrees.[42] When a conservative friar, Caledonio Domeco de Jarauta, led residents of the barrios of Mexico City against the invading U.S. troops in 1847, the moderate ayuntamiento protested to the archbishop.[43] Appeals for mass violence by moderates seem to have been even less common. In 1849 moderate leaders were accused of organizing groups which threw rocks through the windows of conservatives' homes amid a carnival atmosphere complete with fireworks and marching bands.[44]

Moderates and conservatives had more to fear from the rabble and ultimately had more powerful constituencies in the Church, the militias, and the army which made appeals to popular uprising unnecessary and dangerous. Radicals turned to the urban masses because they lacked these alternatives, but they were seldom successful in using urban popular support to take or hold power.

Despite the urban focus of elite politics, the people of Mexico were overwhelmingly rural. Social conflict in rural Mexico had long involved the distribution of property between two institutions, the communal ownership of Indian villages and the private property of the Hispanic population. During the colonial period the crown had used an amalgam of privileges and restrictions to circumscribe and manipulate social groups. Indian communities were granted special privileges and encumbered by special limitations to serve as a counterweight against the power of Spanish landowners, the *hacendados*. The crown attempted to conserve communally owned Indian lands by giving Indians a special juridical status of tutelage and protection. Indians were not allowed to carry arms, ride horses, dress like Spaniards, or leave their villages. While Indians could be forced to repay debts with labor, their lands could not be taken in repayment or forfeited in criminal cases. Alienation of Indian lands was forbidden, and rental agreements were carefully supervised. Communities of Spaniards and Indians were kept separated, and the autonomy of Indian villages was guaranteed.[45] Toward the end of the eighteenth century enlightened liberalism increased pressure to institute small landholding. During the late colonial period various officials and institutions had proposed distribution of communal land and the end of special privileges and restrictions on Indians.[46] The crown attempted to counter the political presence of large landowners by promoting small landholding, especially in the North and along the Gulf coast.[47] A series of peninsular decrees on the subjects of Indians and communal lands culminated with a January 4, 1813, order by the Cortes of Cádiz requiring the division of communally owned agricultural land.[48] Of course, not all decisions of this period were motivated by the spirit of reform. The Consolidación of 1804 included the expropriation of the treasuries of Indian communities to help pay for the defense of Spain.[49] After Independence, national and state governments in Mexico attempted to change rural social relations. Liberals continued their efforts to favor small landholding and legal equality of citizens by attempting to alter the two predominant forms of rural land tenure, the hacienda and the village.

Liberals argued that the special juridical status of Indians and restrictions on their alienation of land were vestiges of colonial domination and racism that were incompatible with the legal equality declared with independence in 1821. Lorenzo de Zavala called colonial restrictions and privileges "a systematized order of oppression" and "a method of domination."[50] Most radicals and moderates recognized that the special juridical status of Indians was rooted in the idea of the Indians' inferiority and hoped to end what they saw as the backwardness of Indian life through education and integration into national society.[51] Civic equality of all citizens was declared in the first federal constitution of 1824 and in every state constitution.[52] Most states regarded communal property as incompatible with individual liberty and abolished the right of villages to own land. Laws abolishing community ownership were passed as early as 1825 in Chihuahua, Jalisco, and Zacatecas; 1826 in Chiapas and Veracruz; 1828 in Puebla and Occidente; 1829 in Michoacán; and 1833 in Mexico.[53]

Radicals and moderates combined awareness of the agrarian problem with some sympathy for the oppressed and dispossessed, but they disagreed on the nature of rural reforms. Francisco García's radical administration in the state of Zacatecas seems to have been the most extreme, requiring division not only of agricultural land (*tierras de común repartimiento*) but the woods, mountain and grazing lands (*ejidos*), and the land on which the village was built (*fundo legal*).[54] In 1851 law in Michoacán excluded streets, plazas, cemeteries, and the rest of the *fundo legal*, but limited the size of private landownership and stipulated that land not be ceded in mortmain. When some villages rebelled the following year, Governor Melchor Ocampo suggested that the division be made voluntary with the state paying all costs and that greater freedom be allowed in the alienation of land.[55] Division seems to have been completed around Guadalajara and some other areas of Jalisco, but results in most of Jalisco, Zacatecas, Occidente, and Veracruz were mixed. In Puebla the division apparently was not enforced, while in Michoacán the law was rescinded.[56]

Moderates typically believed that equal protection of the laws would itself function satisfactorily to insure the improvement of rural social conditions. Some moderates, such as José María Lafragua and Luis de la Rosa, recognized that extraordinarily unequal property distribution contributed to mistreatment of the poor, but moderates contended that radicals such as Ponciano Arriaga, José María Castillo Velasco, Lorenzo de Zavala, and Francisco García were not true liberals since they deviated from the sanctity of private property. De la Rosa argued against the free distribution of land to the poor and insisted that any alteration of rural land tenure take place by distribution through sale without damage to any establishment, corporation, or class.[57]

Radicals regarded large rural estates as obstacles to progress and argued that liberty and productivity required the hacienda be replaced with towns and small properties. Ponciano Arriaga, José María Castillo Velasco, Ignacio Vallarta, Lorenzo de Zavala, Francisco García, and others were more aware of the inequities of rural society. They suggested reforms which offered greater autonomy to local government and would have given more land to those who had none. Ponciano Arriaga argued that legal equality was not sufficient in itself to promote liberty and that, despite the fundamental laws of the land, a privileged caste would be able to establish an aristocracy of wealth and monopolize land and political power. Arriaga proposed that the federal government expropriate parts of nearby haciendas to give to Indians whose villages had no land.[58] On March 29, 1833, the legislature of the state of Mexico decreed the expropriation of property administered by the Philippine Missions. The law included provisions to divide the haciendas into portions sufficient to feed a single family and to distribute the farms to the poor citizens of the state with preference to "Indians and those who had served the cause of Independence and Liberty."[59] While the antipathy of radicals for Church property is well-known, they did not restrict their attacks on large rural estates to those owned by the Church. Lorenzo de Zavala, acting as governor of the state of Mexico, divided lands in the Valley of Toluca among forty Indian villages and convinced the state legislature to expropriate the properties of Cortés's heirs to support public education.[60] Francisco García, a radical governor of the state of Zacatecas, used state funds to buy haciendas and distribute the lands to neighboring communities of small property owners or to convert the haciendas into towns with more equal distributions of lands.[61]

Land divisions also occurred under private initiative. The hacienda of Valparaíso was converted to a town in 1829 when renters promised to pay off the hacienda's creditors; they divided some of the property while holding the rest in common.[62] Francisco Severo Maldonado proposed a national agrarian reform which included a national bank to buy land and sell it in smaller lots at the lowest possible price to as many as possible.[63] In 1846 in the state of Mexico, moderates accused radicals Mariano Arizcorreta, Pedrigón Garay, and Francisco Olaguíbel of conspiring with Santanistas and the militia to take over the state government for the purpose of dividing hacienda lands and giving them away. The plan also allegedly included the sale of Church property and greater intervention in the economy.[64] When Arizcorreta did become governor soon afterward, hacendados complained that he was fomenting discord and criticized his refusal to use troops to return hacienda lands invaded by Indians. Governor Arizcorreta attributed rural unrest to the usurpation of Indian lands and low wages paid by haciendas, and proposed that the state give lands to Indians who had lost theirs.[65] In what is now the state of Guerrero, Juan Alvarez supported Indians in their struggles with hacendados and was able to use this alliance to control a large part of the South.[66]

The destruction of communal land was opposed not by agrarian radicals but by reactionaries and archconservatives who argued that the condition of the Indian masses was worsened by independence and legal equality. Liberals worried that worsened economic conditions would encourage Indians to support reactionary projects to restore the colonial system,[67] and their fears seem to have some foundation in fact. In 1827 Padre Arenas was accused of conspiring to support a Spanish restoration and promising that Indians would regain the privileges and rights they possessed prior to 1808.[68] In 1834 Carlos Tapisteco and Epigmenio de la Picdra, the village priests of Ecatzingo (in what is now the state of Hidalgo), proposed a plan for an Indian monarchy chosen from among the descendants of Moctezuma and promised increased local autonomy and lands for villages without them. Curiously, the plan retained legal equality.[69] Evidence of other reactionary projects is even more limited. Indians attacking the hacienda of Hipala in Jalisco in 1848 reportedly shouted "¡Viva el Emperador!" The parish priest of Zitácuaro, Michoacán, led a rebellion against the division of communal lands in 1851.[70] Later, in the 1850s and 1860s, Indian leaders such as Manuel Lozada in Tepic and the Tánori brothers in Sonora combined support for agrarian justice with support of Maximilian's empire.[71]

Conservatives argued that their concept of racial inferiority had been recognized by Spanish law and justified by the divine plan to civilize and Christianize heathens. Lucas Alamán believed that the generally peaceful rural environment of the colonial period had been produced by Indian submission to priests, low taxation, exemption from military service, and respect for local autonomy of Indian governments. In his view, Indians had been armed and incited to hate Spaniards during the independence wars, and afterward had used violence for their own ends, usurping land belonging to haciendas. Alamán believed that the use of armed force by Indians required their subjugation by superior military force, but he hoped that the general outlines of the colonial order could be restored. He proposed that protective, second-class citizenship be restored to keep Indians from losing their possessions and that the *repúblicas de indios* be reestablished for greater local autonomy. Alamán also wanted to return to the colonial policy of a single personal tax on Indians and to restore the missions in the frontier areas to control wandering tribes.[72]

None of the factions consistently sought support from rural people themselves. Radical plans to end the domination of the countryside by the hacienda and the Indian village were out of touch with the desires of the rural masses, especially those who lived in villages which held communal land. Some radicals advocated the division of hacienda lands, but the actual benefits to the rural poor seem to have been small and were more than outweighed by the radicals' repeated attempts to individualize land tenure in Indian villages. Since the villages had been one of the bases of the colonial order, some conservatives supported the rights of Indians to their traditional land tenure system. Other conservatives sought to save only those vestiges of the colonial heritage which benefited them directly.

No single issue was sufficient to define the political factions of early nineteenth-century Mexico. Federalism and centralism have probably been overrated as a simplification of early political cleavages. What has to be done with power was more important than where power was to be exercised. For example, as governor of the state of Mexico, Lorenzo de Zavala behaved as a federalist and a radical. He agreed with the state legislature on the right of the state government to expropriate Church property. When Vicente Guerrero became president and appointed Zavala his minister of hacienda, Zavala behaved as a centralist radical, hoping to make the expropriation of Church property a national policy but annoying federalist radicals in state government who wanted the state rather than the national government to carry out the expropriation.[73] Later, in writing the Constitution of 1857, Mexican liberals took considerable power away from the states.[74] The religious question can be overstated as well, masking the essential piety of many liberals and the fundamental division of the conservatives between those who were primarily pro-clerical and those, like Santa Anna, who were essentially militarists but also sought a society based on hierarchy, acceptance of inequality, corporate privileges, and state intervention.

Shortly after independence, political factions were not clearly formed. As the first Masonic order in Mexico, the Scottish Rite Masons were a diverse group. Generally considered more conservative than the York Rite Masons, the Scottish lodge nonetheless included men such as Manuel Crescencio Rejón who was known for his radical ideas. As the Masonic lodges faded in importance, there was less formal political organization. David Brading has described Mexican liberalism as a "movement rather than a party" and as a "shifting coalition, a peculiar union of rural caciques and new radicals, of ideologues and the mob."[75] In a similar vein, Lucas Alamán observed that the conservative "party" was "without the form of lodges or any other kind of organization."[76] Political differences polarized after 1848, making moderate positions increasingly untenable. Many moderate liberals grew closer to the conservatives after 1848, fearing national disintegration and social disorder. The reactions to Maximilian's empire were especially revealing of underlying attitudes, but not as a simple dichotomy between republicans and reactionaries. Some of the moderates chose to support the monarchy after it became clear that Maximilian was not himself a reactionary but something of a liberal.[77]

Summarizing an entire political career with a single label inevitably reduces the variations between individuals to a minimum.

Even if misrepresentation of their general positions can be avoided, some of the subtleties of political discourse are invariably lost by using only four general categories. Nevertheless, there are ways to minimize the inevitable ambiguities. First, the individuals included in the statistical analyses which follow were national presidents and cabinet ministers.[78] As prominent politicians, their political positions were generally well-known. In a number of cases it was impossible to classify some individuals as a result of their relative obscurity, and a small number of cases were difficult to classify because of what appears to be capriciousness in adopting political allegiances.[79] I have tried not to push this classification process too far.

Second, ambiguity can be reduced by determining a particular time in the subject's political career when a classification will be made. In cases where some change occurred over time, I have characterized the last position taken while the subject occupied the presidency or one of the ministries. This provides a more difficult test for hypothetical relationships between politics and social or regional origins since accumulated experiences are expected to alter initial predispositions. Socialization should interrupt any congruity between origins and outcomes. In most cases it was not necessary to make such fine temporal distinctions. Since most of the national executive elite served only brief and infrequent terms, they did not enjoy many opportunities to be capricious in their policies.[80]

Finally, these classifications undoubtedly contain errors, but the significance of that fact is subject to interpretation. Historians, like mathematicians, tend to believe that aggregation compounds errors. Our training, our socialization into the historical profession, inclines us to greater faith in individual than collective biography. The approach adopted here is based on a distinct assumption, that is, the standard statistical argument that combining many observations, even though they inevitably contain some errors, results in a more accurate measurement because random errors are symmetrical and cancel each other out.[81]

These descriptions of the major political tendencies in Mexico from independence to the War of the Reform have made up a part of the traditional, that is to say controversial, historiography of Mexico. Some historians will readily accept their significance, and others will dispute them. I submit that either reaction is premature. The remainder of this work tests the utility of these classifications. If some would reject these aggregations, a priori, as misguided, or embrace them immediately as fundamental, readers are advised to remain skeptical and wait to discover whether or not, when confronted with the evidence, these distinctions help explain the instability of early republican Mexico.

Four

Paths to

Power

Those who observed the political struggles of the nineteenth century recognized connections between political factionalism and social divisions. José María Luis Mora, a liberal, saw the struggles of the 1820s as a conflict between progressive politicians in state governments and the reactionary forces of the army and the clergy.[1] Even such a stalwart conservative as Lucas Alamán noted a parallel between social and political conflict. Alamán saw a continuity which linked the Bourbonists and the Scottish Rite Masons of the 1820s, the "Hombres de Bien" of the 1830s, and the group that became known as conservatives in the 1840s. He defined the social basis of this conservative movement as "the Spaniards who were persecuted in the early years of the republic, property owners who wanted security, the clergy who saw their principles attacked, and all of the rest of the classes who wanted tranquility, order, and protection." Later, perhaps in a less expansive mood, Alamán kept his description to "the clergy, the army and all of the propertied class."[2]

There is a long tradition in the history of Mexico which has continued to identify political positions with these broader social divisions of region or class. From Justo Sierra in the early twentieth century to the more recent work of Jesús Reyes Heroles, François Chevalier, and Michael Costeloe, historians have emphasized occupational groups as the key to political divisions. In its simplest form, the argument has been that those who prospered under Spanish rule, the upper ranks of the ecclesiastical and military hierarchies as well as wealthy landowners and merchants, provided the basis for conservative support. Liberals, on the other hand, are generally identified with the lower clergy and military, professionals, and merchants who were victims of monopoly.[3] Richard Sinkin, in his pioneering quantitative study of mid-nineteenth-century Mexican politics, provided some support for identifying liberals with the military and the legal profession. Sinkin found that 67 percent of the delegates to the convention that wrote the Constitution of 1857 were either lawyers or military men.[4]

Despite its long tradition, the hypothesis that political positions coincided with regional and social divisions has not been universally accepted; others have argued that political and social divisions did not overlap. The proposition that social strata and political divisions were not closely related has two main variations. The first is comparatively recent. Since the late 1960s ever-larger numbers of historians of Latin America have proposed that the family rather than the individual is the appropriate unit of analysis.[5] Studies of investment and business interests have noted the tendency of families to diversify their investments, suggesting that those owning substantially the same kinds and amounts of property were likely to have been equally divided on political matters, and that there would be no clear social or property contrasts among political factions. In any event, they argue, politicians were more likely to act in the interest of extended family and diversified businesses rather than narrow individual or political interests.[6] Political conflicts, then, were incidental and personal rather than substantial and structural.

The second thesis is older. For close to fifty years historians have elaborated on hypotheses that the social background of politicians was unrelated to ideology because stated political programs were frivolous disguises for individual ambition; politicians were merely opportunistic caudillos. In this tradition, politics provided an avenue of social mobility for those eager to pillage the treasury. There would be no correlation between social and political divisions, according to this thesis, because caudillos adopted political philosophies to hide their true intentions, and could alter, exchange, or drop these pretenses as the occasion demanded. Social stratification itself, then, was not a real obstacle to individual ambition since violence enabled the caudillo to improve his personal economic position. Entry into the political elite was possible for those of any social background, even the most humble, but leaders from the wealthy classes would be more successful in holding on to power. Wolf and Hansen, for example, contend that most successful leaders would be members of the landed upper class, the *criollo* gentry, who enjoyed preferential access to readily exploitable wealth. Wolf and Hansen argue that governments ruled by caudillos from the poorer classes of Indian or Indian–Spanish parentage, the *mestizos*, would be more unstable than those from the landed *criollo* gentry.

> The *criollo* may be able to draw on his own wealth at the beginning of his undertaking; when liquid wealth grows scarce, he can retrench to provide booty from his own estate. However much a burden this may put on his own resources, it can enable him to weather a period of scarcity, while the *mestizo caudillo* requires continuing abundance.[7]

In theory, access to rural estates might have provided resources which could be used to prolong terms in office, but Mexican observers typically noted that the landed classes did not use their own wealth to promote stability. David Brading has cited the complaints of Carlos María Bustamante and Lucas Alamán that landowners did not participate more actively in government during this unstable period.[8] Others contend that landowners did not participate in national government but exercised their power locally. Francisco López Cámara argued that isolation resulting from long distances and slow communications along with the lack of effective government made owners of large haciendas the "absolute lords" of their domains who after independence exploited their workers and enjoyed "absolute dominion over the lands they owned."[9] Frank Safford has argued that rural landowners had no special interests in government since few issues directly concerned them other than the condition of roads or the acquisition of land. If government was essentially irrelevant, hacendados would avoid politics.[10] Richard Graham has suggested that the absence of landowners in government offices was responsible for instability. "We could posit that the more regularly landowners took a direct and daily interest in the affairs of government at the national level, the more stable were resulting regimes."[11]

The hypothetical relationship between access to rural wealth and political stability is shaky at best, and the suggestion that rural

Table 4.1   Educational Categories by Political Factions

	Law	Mili-tary	Law and Mili-tary	Church	Medi-cine	Science and Engi-neering	Un-known	Total
Radicals	14 (24%)	15 (25%)	3 (5%)	0 (0%)	3 (5%)	2 (3%)	22 (37%)	59
Moderates	23 (34%)	22 (32%)	3 (4%)	3 (4%)	0 (0%)	0 (0%)	17 (25%)	68
Conser-vatives	26 (25%)	35 (34%)	1 (1%)	5 (5%)	0 (0%)	5 (5%)	30 (29%)	102
Total	62	72	7	8	3	7	69	229

Statistics: Cramer's $V = 0.216$. Chi-square $= 21.349$ with 12 degrees of freedom (DF). Probability $= 0.0455$.
Notes: Some rows may not total 100 percent due to rounding.
Sources: See Appendix A.

landowners' lack of participation in government caused instability cannot be subject to empirical investigation at all. Wealthy landowners are presumed to have held potential political power and to have chosen not to exercise that power. In practice, it would be impossible to distinguish between those hypothetically astute landowners who allegedly held the solution to stable government from those landowners who were merely politically impotent despite their wealth. Nonparticipation makes these landowners politically invisible and specifies a counterfactual analysis that cannot be tested empirically. It is more practical to study the variation among those who did choose to participate in government to see whether those more successful in gaining and maintaining power differed in important ways from their less successful counterparts.

Table 4.1 presents cross-tabulations of political groups with occupational categories for 229 men who occupied the presidency or one of the cabinet ministries between 1824 and 1867.[12] Over 60 percent of the total were either lawyers or military officers. Moderates show a slightly greater preference for the law, and moderates and conservatives were more likely to be military officers, but the differences between the factions are not very large. Nearly a third of the moderates claimed a law degree compared with a quarter of the radicals and conservatives. About 36 percent of the moderates and conservatives held military commissions, while 30 percent of the radicals were army or militia officers.[13]

These figures, by themselves, do not indicate large differences between political factions in education and training. Although greater numbers and higher percentages of moderates and conservatives than radicals pursued careers in the Church and military, soldiers and priests were a minority of each group. Although radicals were more likely to have occupations outside military and ecclesiastical hierarchies, the variations displayed in this table are subject to four limitations and qualifications.

First, such tables do not directly test the hypothesis of political support by different occupational groups. Instead, they test the relationship between occupational categories and political ideas only for an elite of presidents and cabinet ministers. Rather than testing for political differences between a group of colonels and generals, for example, it attempts to find differences in political affiliations between generals who achieved political power.

Second, there is a tendency to regard occupation as a discrete category, while individuals are more likely to be involved in various ways of earning a living. A man with a law degree might also own property or engage in trade. The problem is one of identification. Nearly all of the occupational categories in table 4.1 use a professional title, whether *licenciado*, *general*, *fray*, *padre*, *dóctor*, or *ingeniero*. Table 4.1 is more accurately a cross-tabulation of professional titles used by politicians rather than a precise listing of their occupations. Such categories are probably a better indication of education than occupation.

Third, occupation and education may be insignificant in assessing political differences since, by the time one reaches the pinnacle of political power, he has already attained some wealth and education.[14] Not only are professional titles more likely to be noticed than other occupational categories, but training in law or the military was more likely to give a politician the training and affiliations he needed to achieve a powerful post, no matter what his goals might be in the use of that power. The process of attaining a position may be more significant than the position attained. Occupation has been used as a proxy for more interesting variables on social origins and career paths. Seen in this light, perhaps the fundamental statistic in table 4.1 is that 75 percent of the moderates and 71 percent of the conservatives (but only 63 percent of the radicals) used a professional title. Again, this is probably not so important for what it indicates about occupation as what it may indicate about education and social origins.[15]

Fourth, this cross-tabulation makes the unwarranted assumption that individual experiences within each of these categories were fundamentally the same, when we know that this was clearly not the case.[16] Take the military, for example. The Mexican army after independence was divided between those who had been insurgents and those who had been royalists during the wars of the independence era. When these forces came together as the Army of the Three Guarantees that marched into Mexico City on September 27, 1821, it was composed of former antagonists from distinct regions and social backgrounds. At the front of the column of some 16,000 men rode Agustín de Iturbide, a royalist officer who only recently had converted to the cause of independence. With his light skin, precise uniform, and elegant movements, Iturbide struck poses on a large black horse, causing a poet to remark that he appeared "as arrogant as a statue." The refined creole officer pretended to disdain the crowd's applause. Popular enthusiasm rose to delirium, however, when they saw the troops led by Vicente Guerrero. Where Iturbide was haughty, Guerrero's men were justifiably proud of fighting without a truce for eleven years, proud of their ragged clothes and bare feet, proud of their antiquated equipment, and proud of their dark skins.[17]

The old animosities had been set aside, or so it seemed. Even though Iturbide had been their enemy for a decade, Guerrero's troops may have hoped he had converted to their cause. The Plan of Iguala united the Mexican elite in apparent consensus, but the agreement was tenuous. The social backgrounds of Guerrero and Iturbide illustrate the deep differences between the factions which had fought for and against independence prior to Iguala. Despite its broad support for the Plan of Iguala, Iturbide was well-aware that his army was not a unified force; he used promotions to increase the power of his supporters and limit the strength of his enemies. Iturbide gave control of the army to Pedro Celestino Negrete, a conservative Spaniard. Of five field marshals, only one was a former insurgent, while ten of the eleven brigadier generals were former royalist officers. Enlisted men who had fought against the insurgents were raised one to four grades in rank, but Guerrero's guerrillas were not promoted.[18]

Table 4.2   Postindependence Political Factions by Independence
Era Activity

	Active	Inactive	Total
Radicals	10 (63%)	6 (37%)	16
Moderates	19 (56%)	15 (44%)	34
Conservatives	21 (64%)	12 (36%)	33
Total	50	33	83

Statistics: Cramer's V = 0.075. Chi-square = 0.462 with 2 DF. Probability = 0.794.
Notes: "Active" includes all those who participated in the struggles between 1808 and 1821 whether as insurgents or royalists, militants, conspirators, or propagandists. "Inactive" includes those who pursued their educations or occupations without becoming involved in the controversy.
Sources: See Appendix A.

Most of the presidents and cabinet ministers who served from the beginning of the First Federal Republic in 1824 to the end of Maximilian's empire in 1867 were born before Guerrero and Iturbide joined their forces together. Nearly half were old enough to have taken part in the events of that era, some of them at very young ages. Benito Quijano, for example, became a cadet in the Spanish army at the age of twelve. Tables 4.2 and 4.3 include all of the postindependence political elite who were born prior to 1800 or known to have taken an active role for or against the insurgency prior to Iturbide's coalition with Guerrero. Of this cohort, a majority of those in each postindependence faction were active participants, but a substantial portion of each group took no militant position on the question of independence. Thirty-seven percent of the postindependence radicals were involved solely with their own affairs during these crucial years, as were 44 percent of the moderates and 36 percent of the conservatives. Francisco García Salinas, later a radical, was occupied in the mining business in Zacatecas. José Gómez de la Cortina, later a conservative, spent much of the time studying in Spain. Manuel de la Peña y Peña, later a moderate, worked quietly in the colonial administration in Mexico City. Postindependence radicals and conservatives took militant roles with slightly greater frequency than did moderates, but the differences in proportions between the three groups are not statistically significant.

If none of the factions was especially notable for its militancy, table 4.3 demonstrates that there were significant differences among those who did take up arms. Radicals and conservatives were most likely to have found themselves on opposite sides during the wars for independence. Prior to the Plan of Iguala, radicals were more likely than moderates or conservatives to have fought for independence. Seven of the ten active radicals sided with the insurgent movement; the only exceptions were three cadets, two of whom were born far from the principal areas of insurgent activity: Pedro Ampudia, born in Cuba in 1805; Benito Quijano, born in Yucatán in 1800; and José Ignacio Basadre, born in Veracruz in 1799. Conservatives were most likely to have joined local militias or the Spanish army to fight against the insurgents. Eighty-four percent of the conservatives who took a militant position on independence had been royalists. If radicals and conservatives were likely to hold consistent positions before and after Iguala, moderates were almost evenly divided by the use of violence to achieve independence. Of those who took up arms, 44 percent of the postindependence moderates had been insurgents, while 56 percent fought with the royalists. The moderates were split between those who supported the constitutional process under way in Spain and those who supported armed insurrection in Mexico.

Among those who began their military careers after independence, a similar correlation holds between political philosophy and military experience. Table 4.4 shows a strong and statistically significant relationship between political factions and distinct types of military units. Radicals regarded the national army as ineffective,

Table 4.3   Postindependence Political Factions by Independence Era Factions

	Insurgents	Royalists	Total
Radicals	7 (70%)	3 (30%)	10
Moderates	8 (44%)	11 (56%)	19
Conservatives	4 (16%)	17 (84%)	21
Total	19	31	50

Statistics: Cramer's $V = 0.392$. Chi-square $= 7.684$ with 2 DF. Probability $= 0.0215$.
Sources: See Appendix A.

Table 4.4   Political Factions by Initial Military Experience, 1822–1867

	State or Civic Militia	National Army	Total
Radicals	11 (100%)	0 (0%)	11
Moderates	2 (40%)	3 (60%)	5
Conservatives	1 (10%)	9 (90%)	10
Total	14	12	26

Statistics: Cramer's V = 0.822. Chi-square = 17.55 with 2 DF. Probability = 0.0002.
Sources: See Appendix A and Alberto M. Carreño, *Jefes de ejército mexicano en 1847* (Mexico: Secretaría de Fomento, 1914), supplemented with information from *Diccionario Porrúa de historia, biografía, y geografía de México*, 3 vols., 5th ed. (Mexico: Editorial Porrúa, 1986), and Alberto Leduc, Luís Lara y Pardo, and Carlos Roumagnac, *Diccionario de geografía, historia y biografía mexicanas* (Paris: Librería de la Vda. de Ch. Bouret, 1910).

corrupt, tyrannical, and reactionary. They sought to buttress the national defense with forces of civilian soldiers during the war with the United States in 1847 and to use civic and state militias as an alternative to the national army. All of the radical cabinet ministers and presidents who began their military careers after 1821 started in these irregular forces, national guards, and civic militias. Conservatives regarded these units as irresponsible rabble and a potential threat to the power of the national army. All but one of the conservatives who began military careers after independence joined the national army; the single exception, Félix Zuloaga, began his career far from the national capital in the provincial militia of Chihuahua.

Radicals, moderates, and conservatives were likely to follow different paths to national power; they began their political careers in different sorts of positions. Information about presidents and cabinet ministers was collated with records of national senators and congressional deputies from 1821 to 1857[19] and state governors after 1821.[20] Table 4.5 demonstrates significant differences in the first important political posts held by radicals, moderates, and conservatives. Political career patterns varied with political philosophy. Liberals, whether moderates or radicals, tended to begin their political careers in the national legislature. Half of the radicals and more than 60 percent of the moderates began their careers in the national legislature, which may indicate their conviction that compromise, conciliation, collective resolution, and the rule of law could be used to solve the nation's problems. The national legislature was clearly a training ground for liberal politicians.

Conservatives, in contrast, tended to begin their careers in positions of executive authority, especially in the national executive, suggesting a more active, directive orientation toward government. While liberals were more likely to begin as legislators, conservatives were more likely to start in executive posts at the cabinet level or the presidency. Two-thirds of the conservatives began in executive offices, indicating that conservatives were less likely than moderates and radicals to have previous governmental experience before holding office as presidents or cabinet ministers. About half of all conservatives began their careers in the nation's highest executive offices without first serving in the national legislature or as a state governor. In contrast, three-quarters of the radicals and moderates had legislative or state gubernatorial experience before becoming cabinet ministers or presidents.

A small minority of politicians from each faction began their political careers as state governors, but the radicals were more likely to serve as executives on the state level before taking office as president or cabinet minister. Nearly a quarter of the radicals (24 percent) began their pursuit of power in the state capitals compared to only 15 percent of the conservatives and 12 percent of the moderates. The national executive elite was filled predominantly with men who had enough influence to propel themselves directly into the national legislature or the cabinet ministries, but radicals were

Table 4.5 Political Factions by First Major Political Post, 1821–1867

	State Governor	National Legislator	National Executive	Total
Radicals	14 (24%)	30 (51%)	15 (25%)	59
Moderates	8 (12%)	42 (62%)	18 (26%)	68
Conservatives	15 (15%)	37 (36%)	50 (49%)	102
Total	37	109	83	229

Statistics: Cramer's V = 0.193. Chi-square = 17.075 with 4 DF. Probability = 0.0019.
Notes: Some rows may not total 100 percent due to rounding.
Sources: See Appendix A.

more likely than moderates or conservatives to begin as state governors.

Within the groups of radicals and conservatives, a military commission made a difference in career patterns, as shown in table 4.6. Radical officers more frequently began their political careers as state governors than their civilian cohorts. Civilian radicals were more likely to serve in the national legislature and more often were appointed to cabinet positions without previous experience as state governors or national legislators. Among conservatives, the opposite pattern prevailed. Conservative civilians often had experience as state governors before joining the national executive elite, while conservative army officers more frequently became cabinet ministers and presidents without previous experience at other government levels. Almost all of the conservatives who began military careers after 1821 were regular army officers. Conservative officers made up more than two-thirds of all military officers who began their careers in the national executive elite, illustrating the strong relationship that has been described between the upper echelons of the national army and the conservative party. Although approximately equal percentages of each group were made up of military officers, the officers in each group typically began their careers in different branches of government, the radicals in state governorships, moderates as national legislators, and conservatives as presidents and cabinet ministers.

These results show statistically significant relationships between career paths and political programs. Occupation and formal education tell us much less about the relationship between experience and outlook than patterns of military participation and political careers.

Radicals were likely to have fought for independence from Spain and to have joined the state and civic militias that competed for power with the national army. Radicals with military training often were state governors and national legislators in their first important political posts. Civilian radicals began their careers most often in the national legislature.

Many moderates were active in the wars of the independence era, but moderates were divided on the use of violence to achieve separation from Spain. Some moderates fought with the insurgents, but more joined the royalists. After 1821, moderates seldom

Table 4.6 Political Factions by First Major Political Office for
Civilians and Military, 1821–1867

	State Governor		National Legislator		National Executive		
	Civilian	Military	Civilian	Military	Civilian	Military	Total
Radicals	5 (8%)	9 (15%)	24 (41%)	6 (10%)	12 (20%)	3 (5%)	59
Moderates	4 (6%)	4 (6%)	27 (40%)	15 (22%)	12 (18%)	6 (9%)	68
Conservatives	8 (8%)	7 (7%)	26 (25%)	11 (11%)	32 (31%)	18 (18%)	102
Total	17	20	77	32	56	27	229

Statistics: Cramer's $V = 0.218$. Chi-square $= 21.825$ with 10 DF. Probability $= 0.0160$.
Notes: Some rows may not total 100 percent due to rounding.
Sources: See Appendix A.

chose to lead military forces, whether national, state, or civic.
Whether or not they had been military officers, moderates were
most likely to take up positions in the congress; nearly two-thirds
served in the national legislature before becoming presidents or cabinet ministers.

Conservatives bore arms against the insurgents in 1810 and
fought for Spain until Iturbide used independence to avoid resurgent Spanish liberalism. After independence, conservatives were
more likely to take up careers in the national army than in the militias. Nearly half of the conservatives, including half of the conservative officers, started their careers in the executive elite without
previous experience in the state capitals or national legislature. Civilian conservatives were likely to have participated in the national
legislature but in smaller proportions than the liberals. Few conservatives were state governors prior to becoming president or being
charged with a cabinet ministry.

These correlations may tell us something about the origins of
instability. Some of the conflict between radicals and conservatives
is rooted in the struggles of insurgents and royalists during the wars
of independence. In part, the origins of the leadership of these three
factions in distinct military experiences and political offices demonstrates the moderates' potential to mediate between the radicals
and the conservatives. Moderates bridged the factions of the independence era, fighting for both the insurgents and the royalists before Iturbide brought the two sides together. After independence,

moderates seldom took up military careers and most often began their political careers in the legislature, that branch of government that most depends on compromise and conciliation. These observations suggest that moderates with experience in the congress may well have held the most potential to lead stable governments in early republican Mexico.

Five

Holding on to

Power

During the first decades after independence, presidents replaced one another at a dizzying pace. From the birth of the First Mexican Republic in 1824 to the outbreak of the War of the Reform in 1857, Mexico had sixteen presidents and thirty-three provisional national leaders, a total of forty-nine administrations in thirty-three years. Even within these presidencies there was little consistency of administration. Cabinet secretaries were shuffled at an even more furious pace; the same thirty-three years saw the war ministry change hands fifty-three times, the foreign ministry fifty-seven times, the justice ministry sixty-one times, and the finance ministry eighty-seven times (see table 5.1).[1] Government officials at any level might last no longer than a few days, and only rarely did they last for more than two or three years.

Given the prevailing instability, what personal characteristics might have ameliorated the instability and prolonged political careers? Instability may have been affected by at least three related but analytically distinct factors, which may be termed politics, experience, and origins.

Political differences may have contributed to short terms in office. Extreme political positions were probably more likely to result in conflict than were moderate philosophies and policies. Those who demanded change might have been forced out of office more quickly than those who were content with the status quo. Presidents and cabinet ministers who chose to collaborate with the

Table 5.1   Statistics for Executive Elite Lengths of Term, 1824–1857

Position	N	Mean Months	Minimum Months	Maximum Months	SD
President	16	12.81	0	54	15.07
Minister of War	53	6.32	0	30	7.04
Minister of Finance	87	4.31	0	35	5.80
Foreign Minister	57	4.98	0	32	6.18
Minister of Justice	61	6.13	0	29	6.59
Provisional President	33	5.97	0	32	8.11
Provisional War	24	2.12	0	21	4.48
Provisional Finance	32	0.75	0	3	0.92
Provisional Foreign	28	3.07	0	20	5.27
Provisional Justice	33	1.24	0	14	2.51
Total	424	4.65	0	54	6.82

economic elites might have served longer terms than those who proposed changing the prevailing system.

Experience may have played a role as well. Presidents and cabinet ministers assumed office after different types of seasoning in government. Some had been governors or representatives to the national congress. Many had previously been in charge of a cabinet ministry or even the presidency itself. All of these positions might reasonably have provided advantages which would enable those with previous political practice to endure longer terms in office than those without administrative or legislative backgrounds. Earlier experiences might have been important in preparing leaders for positions in government. Were university and military training helpful in socializing individuals or creating networks of men that would prolong political terms? Education may have acquainted these executives with Mexico's legal traditions, cultivated more rational administrative policies, or taught communication skills useful in government service. Military service might have provided experience in leadership; or perhaps access to the military's coercive power provided advantages to officers over presidents and cabinet ministers without such education or military experience.

Children from a variety of geographic regions and social backgrounds may have shared experiences in the university or the military, but earlier conditions in life could have fundamentally influenced the opportunities and obstacles they later encountered. Birthplace may be a useful proxy for other social background variables which are difficult to study directly. Those born in the national or state capitals may have had advantages in social connections and access to education that enabled them to hold on to power longer than those whose origins were in rural areas and towns without considerable administrative apparatus.[2] Assigning weights to each of these factors would be a significant step toward determining the relationship between social origins, individual experience, and politics in causing instability. If these sources of instability can be distinguished from one another, we could determine whether or not instability was rooted in the conflicts between social or regional groups, whether or not more education and experience might have prolonged political careers, and whether political differences contributed to the difficulties after independence or whether political labels were largely irrelevant.

Certainly in the lifetime of an individual the three factors of origin, experience, and political position are likely to be closely related. The material conditions of a child's family are likely to constrain the opportunities available to that child, and the combination of origins and experiences may well result in congruent political principles. On the other hand, if educational and career opportunities are not limited in any way by geography or family circumstances, political ideas are likely to be more closely correlated with education and experience than with social or regional origins.

Analytically sorting out these multiple hypothetical sources of political instability is only the beginning of the problem. Many of these theoretical categories tend to coincide in fact. Origins and experience overlapped with politics; radicals, moderates, and conservatives tended to come from distinct types of cities and to begin their careers in different posts.[3] Some had a university education, others were trained in the military. Radicals with military experience were more likely to have started their careers as state governors. Conservatives with military experience were less likely to have experience in legislatures or state governorships. How much variation in lengths of terms may be due to legislative experience and how much to the fact that many former legislators were political moderates?

Traditional narrative history has been unable to encompass these complexities of political turbulence, but a multivariate statistical technique can distinguish among the effects of numerous variables and describe the general structure of political instability's individual components. Analysis of variance is a statistical technique that compares the effects of independent categorical divisions (called "factors") of a group on a continuous dependent variable measured at the interval level (in this case the lengths of terms as president or cabinet minister). In other words, by distinguishing among group means, analysis of variance can determine which groups tended to have distinctly different abilities to hold on to power.[4] The relative explanatory strength of these variables can be evaluated by including them in the analysis. In the following analyses of variance, variables will be added to the calculations to compare aspects of sociogeographic background, education, administrative experience, and political positions which might be expected to affect an individual's ability to prolong his political service.[5]

Analysis of variance compares the means of subgroups as deviations from the overall average, known as the "grand mean." In table 5.2, group means for presidents and each of the cabinet ministries are expressed as deviations from the grand mean of 6.09 months. Adding the deviations for each group to the grand mean gives an average length of term for that group. In each of the following tables the first column of deviations (labeled "Unadjusted Deviation") shows how much the group deviates from the grand mean without considering the compounding effects of other variables. Since we are principally interested in assessing precisely the differing effects of these variables, the discussion which follows refers to the second column of deviations (labeled "Adjusted for Independents Deviation") which separates out the overlapping effects of the other variables included in each analysis. Comparing these deviations and group means allows a more precise measurement of instability and the influences of various sorts of politics, experiences, and origins on that instability.

The results indicate that variations in position, birthplace, and politics are significant sources of instability. Presidents were more likely to hold office for longer periods than cabinet ministers. Presidents averaged about fifteen months in office compared to about seven for ministers of war or justice, and less than five months for

Table 5.2   Analysis of Variance of Lengths of Term by Position, Politics, Birthplace, and Title

Grand Mean = 6.09		Unadjusted		Adjusted for Independents	
Variable + Category	N	Deviation	Eta	Deviation	Beta
Position					
1 President	16	6.72		8.76	
2 Minister of War	46	0.54		0.91	
3 Minister of Finance	74	−1.51		−1.37	
4 Foreign Relations	56	−1.02		−1.84	
5 Minister of Justice	45	0.80		0.49	
			0.27		0.34
Politics					
1 Radical	39	−2.65		−3.06	
2 Moderate	98	1.34		1.66	
3 Conservative	69	0.09		0.73	
4 Santanista	31	−1.09		−3.03	
			0.19		0.26
Birthplace					
1 Mexico City	49	−2.56		−2.64	
2 Provincial Capital	60	1.46		2.39	
3 Other Town	77	0.07		−0.44	
4 Rural	51	0.64		0.38	
			0.19		0.23
Title					
1 Professional	108	−0.26		0.45	
2 Military	76	1.58		−0.61	
3 Neither	53	−1.75		−0.04	
			0.16		0.06

Statistics:

Source of Variation	Sum of Squares	DF	Mean Square	F	Significance of F
Main Effects	2351.119	12	195.927	3.882	0.000
Position	1000.195	4	250.049	4.954	0.001
Politics	827.835	3	275.945	5.467	0.001
Birthplace	677.272	3	225.757	4.473	0.005
Title	19.417	2	9.709	0.192	0.825
Explained	2351.119	12	195.927	3.882	0.000
Residual	11306.020	224	50.473		
Total	13657.139	236	57.869		

Multiple R Squared = 0.172.
Multiple R   = 0.415.

finance and foreign relations ministers. Extreme political positions often resulted in instability. Radical liberals and the personal clique of militarist Antonio López de Santa Anna were more likely to serve very brief terms than moderates and conservatives. Moderates averaged the longest terms at 7.66 months. Conservatives served mean terms of about 6.82 months, with radicals and Santanistas leaving office after only about three months.

Those born in the national capital enjoyed no apparent advantages in prolonged terms and held office for terms shortened by about 2.64 months. Presidents and cabinet ministers from rural backgrounds and towns without substantial state or national administrations were likely to serve nearly average terms, while those from state or provincial capitals averaged terms longer by 2.39 months. Social origin seems to have played a larger and more fundamental role in determining political longevity than socialization. Long-term possibilities, as indicated by birthplace, had a larger effect than more immediate sources of advantage such as education and training. University education and military training were largely insignificant when these other aspects of origins and experience are considered; deviations from the grand mean are small, and the results are statistically insignificant at acceptable levels.

This overall result is consistent through a whole series of different ways of assessing experience. In tables 5.3 through 5.6, different types of executive and legislative experience are added in place of education and military training. In table 5.3, previous experience in the same post is associated with changes in mean length of term that are both extremely small and statistically insignificant. In table 5.4, previous experience in other posts in the national executive elite also failed to prolong subsequent terms or to meet standards of statistical significance. Nor was experience as a state governor likely to increase stability. Former governors actually served shorter terms than those without such experience, a statistically significant result at the 0.05 level. Table 5.5 shows that former governors averaged terms 2.4 months shorter than those who had not served as state executives. Legislative experience, on the other hand, tended to prolong individual terms in office. Table 5.6 indicates that former legislators lasted more than two months longer on the average than those without such experience.

Lengths of individual terms are but one measure of political

Table 5.3   Analysis of Variance of Lengths of Term by Position,
Politics, Birthplace, and Experience in the Same Position

Grand Mean = 6.09		Unadjusted		Adjusted for Independents	
Variable + Category	N	Deviation	Eta	Deviation	Beta
Position					
1 President	16	6.72		8.21	
2 Minister of War	46	0.54		0.35	
3 Minister of Finance	74	− 1.51		− 1.34	
4 Foreign Relations	56	− 1.02		− 1.52	
5 Minister of Justice	45	0.80		0.81	
			0.27		0.32
Politics					
1 Radical	39	− 2.65		− 3.07	
2 Moderate	98	1.34		1.64	
3 Conservative	69	0.09		0.72	
4 Santanista	31	− 1.09		− 2.93	
			0.19		0.26
Birthplace					
1 Mexico City	49	− 2.56		− 2.58	
2 Provincial Capital	60	1.46		2.41	
3 Other Town	77	0.07		− 0.44	
4 Rural	51	0.64		0.31	
			0.19		0.23
Experience in Same Position					
0 No	137	0.08		0.13	
1 Yes	100	− 0.11		− 0.17	
			0.01		0.02

Statistics:

Source of Variation	Sum of Squares	DF	Mean Square	F	Significance of F
Main Effects	2336.449	11	212.404	4.222	0.000
Position	1165.904	4	291.476	5.793	0.000
Politics	851.828	3	283.943	5.643	0.001
Birthplace	656.812	3	218.937	4.351	0.005
Same position	4.748	1	4.748	0.094	0.759
Explained	2336.449	11	212.404	4.222	0.000
Residual	11320.690	225	50.314		
Total	13657.139	236	57.869		

Multiple R Squared = 0.171.
Multiple R   = 0.414.

Table 5.4   Analysis of Variance of Lengths of Term by Position, Politics, Birthplace, and Experience in the Executive Elite

Grand Mean = 6.09

Variable + Category	N	Unadjusted		Adjusted for Independents	
		Deviation	Eta	Deviation	Beta
Position					
1 President	16	6.72		8.46	
2 Minister of War	46	0.54		0.15	
3 Minister of Finance	74	−1.51		−1.34	
4 Foreign Relations	56	−1.02		−1.40	
5 Minister of Justice	45	0.80		0.78	
			0.27		0.32
Politics					
1 Radical	39	−2.65		−3.25	
2 Moderate	98	1.34		1.68	
3 Conservative	69	0.09		0.70	
4 Santanista	31	−1.09		−2.78	
			0.19		0.27
Birthplace					
1 Mexico City	49	−2.56		−2.59	
2 Provincial Capital	60	1.46		2.32	
3 Other Town	77	0.07		−0.40	
4 Rural	51	0.64		0.35	
			0.19		0.22
Experience in Executive Elite					
0 No	104	0.50		0.78	
1 Yes	133	−0.39		−0.61	
			0.06		0.09

Statistics: Source of Variation	Sum of Squares	DF	Mean Square	F	Significance of F
Main effects	2435.423	11	221.402	4.439	0.000
Position	1200.895	4	300.224	6.020	0.000
Politics	880.831	3	293.610	5.887	0.001
Birthplace	641.114	3	213.705	4.285	0.006
Executive Elite	103.721	1	103.721	2.080	0.151
Explained	2435.423	11	221.402	4.439	0.000
Residual	11221.717	225	49.874		
Total	13657.139	236	57.869		

Multiple R Squared = 0.178.
Multiple R   = 0.422.

Table 5.5   Analysis of Variance of Lengths of Term by Position,
Politics, Birthplace, and Experience as State Governor

Grand Mean = 6.09

Variable + Category	N	Unadjusted		Adjusted for Independents	
		Deviation	Eta	Deviation	Beta
Position					
1 President	16	6.72		9.17	
2 Minister of War	46	0.54		0.86	
3 Minister of Finance	74	−1.51		−1.65	
4 Foreign Relations	56	−1.02		−1.68	
5 Minister of Justice	45	0.80		0.66	
			0.27		0.36
Politics					
1 Radical	39	−2.65		−2.94	
2 Moderate	98	1.34		1.46	
3 Conservative	69	0.09		0.77	
4 Santanista	31	−1.09		−2.62	
			0.19		0.24
Birthplace					
1 Mexico City	49	−2.56		−2.65	
2 Provincial Capital	60	1.46		2.31	
3 Other Town	77	0.07		−0.34	
4 Rural	51	0.64		0.34	
			0.19		0.22
Experience as State Governor					
0 No	180	0.18		0.58	
1 Yes	57	−0.58		−1.82	
			0.04		0.14

Statistics:

Source of Variation	Sum of Squares	DF	Mean Square	F	Significance of F
Main Effects	2523.715	11	229.429	4.637	0.000
Position	1342.713	4	335.678	6.784	0.000
Politics	719.021	3	239.674	4.844	0.003
Birthplace	651.353	3	217.118	4.388	0.005
State Governor	192.013	1	192.013	3.880	0.050
Explained	2523.715	11	229.429	4.637	0.000
Residual	11133.425	225	49.482		
Total	13657.139	236	57.869		

Multiple R Squared = 0.185.
Multiple R   = 0.430.

Table 5.6   Analysis of Variance of Lengths of Term by Position, Politics, Birthplace, and Experience in the Legislature

Grand Mean = 6.09		Unadjusted		Adjusted for Independents	
Variable + Category	N	Deviation	Eta	Deviation	Beta
Position					
1 President	16	6.72		9.31	
2 Minister of War	46	0.54		0.20	
3 Minister of Finance	74	−1.51		−1.26	
4 Foreign Relations	56	−1.02		−1.60	
5 Minister of Justice	45	0.80		0.55	
			0.27		0.35
Politics					
1 Radical	39	−2.65		−3.40	
2 Moderate	98	1.34		1.49	
3 Conservative	69	0.09		1.29	
4 Santanista	31	−1.09		−3.31	
			0.19		0.29
Birthplace					
1 Mexico City	49	−2.56		−2.46	
2 Provincial Capital	60	1.46		2.51	
3 Other Town	77	0.07		−0.29	
4 Rural	51	0.64		−0.16	
			0.19		0.22
Experience in Legislature					
0 No	100	−0.70		−1.45	
1 Yes	137	0.51		1.10	
			0.08		0.17

Statistics: Source of Variation	Sum of Squares	DF	Mean Square	F	Significance of F
Main effects	2631.793	11	239.254	4.883	0.000
Position	1351.728	4	337.932	6.896	0.000
Politics	994.648	3	331.549	6.766	0.000
Birthplace	649.899	3	216.633	4.421	0.005
Legislature	300.091	1	300.091	6.124	0.014
Explained	2631.793	11	239.254	4.883	0.000
Residual	11025.346	225	49.002		
Total	13657.139	236	57.869		

Multiple R Squared = 0.193.
Multiple R   = 0.439.

success. Since most terms were short, perhaps the total length of time that an individual occupied various important government posts would be appropriate. In post-World War II France and Italy the upper levels of the political elite were volatile; politicians left posts frequently, but cabinet instability was balanced by the probability that any individual would soon occupy another position and have a relatively long career in multiple offices. But in nineteenth-century Mexico, both the lengths of individual terms and the lengths of political careers were likely to be short. The length of entire careers in the national executive elite averaged only ten months (see table 5.7). Half of the presidents and cabinet ministers during this period held these important executive offices for four months or less. Three-quarters served twelve months or less, while 94 percent held top executive posts no more than three years during those three decades. Clearly, most of these national politicians spent comparatively little time in office and served on only a few occasions.

Table 5.8 displays the results of an analysis of variance of total lengths of careers in important executive posts.[6] These results help put the previous analyses in context. The factors that prolonged individual terms were not always likely to promote an extended career, but moderate political positions lengthened individual terms as well as political careers. Moderates not only were likely to serve individual terms longer than those of conservatives or radicals, but they were more likely to have longer careers. Political moderates averaged 1.5 months longer in their careers than conservatives and twelve months longer than radicals. Prominent radicals were generally least successful in extending their political careers; the average length of time radicals spent in the national executive branch was less than four months, a career average shorter than the overall mean for individual terms in office. Those associated with Santa Anna averaged careers six months longer than the overall average despite the fact that their individual terms tended to be shorter than average. Although the Santanistas were a tiny minority of all who held office in this era, their tendency to repeatedly hold power very briefly has attracted historians' attention and has exaggerated the extent of political instability in these years.

Education and military training appear to have had some effect on the probability of extending a political career. Education in law, medicine, or the Church is associated with a total career in office

Table 5.7   Frequencies of Total Months in National
Offices, 1824–1857

Total Months	Frequency	Percentage	Cumulative Percentage
0	36	17.0	17.0
1	30	14.2	31.1
2	12	5.7	36.8
3	16	7.5	44.3
4	13	6.1	50.5
5	11	5.2	55.7
6	8	3.8	59.4
7	9	4.2	63.7
8	6	2.8	66.5
9	4	1.9	68.4
10	8	3.8	72.2
11	2	.9	73.1
12	4	1.9	75.0
13	1	.5	75.5
14	1	.5	75.9
15	2	.9	76.9
16	6	2.8	79.7
17	5	2.4	82.1
18	1	.5	82.5
19	2	.9	83.5
20	3	1.4	84.9
22	1	.5	85.4
23	2	.9	86.3
24	1	.5	86.8
25	3	1.4	88.2
26	2	.9	89.2
27	2	.9	90.1
28	1	.5	90.6
29	2	.9	91.5
31	1	.5	92.0
32	1	.5	92.5
33	1	.5	92.9
34	1	.5	93.4
35	1	.5	93.9
36	1	.5	94.3
40	3	1.4	95.8

Table 5.7 (continued)

Total Months	Frequency	Percentage	Cumulative Percentage
52	1	.5	96.2
54	1	.5	96.7
55	1	.5	97.2
63	1	.5	97.6
67	2	.9	98.6
71	1	.5	99.1
72	1	.5	99.5
81	1	.5	100.0
	211	100.0	

Statistics: Mean = 10.2 months. Mode = 0.0 months. Median = 4.0 months. SD = 14.9 months.

about two weeks shorter than the overall average. The lack of university education or military training seems to have decreased time in office by more than three months compared to the grand mean and nearly six months compared to the mean for military officers. Military officers served longer during their political careers than university graduates and those without professional titles, but the length of their individual terms was nearly average.[7] Frequent terms of only average length for military officers indicate that ties to the military forces helped them gain power but did not help them sustain it.

Instability does not have the expected relationship to the geographic origins of politicians. Presidents and cabinet ministers born in Mexico City not only served shorter individual terms, but they were likely to serve fewer total months in the national executive elite. Natives of Mexico City averaged a little less than half of the grand mean, a total of about six months during their lifetimes. Presidents and cabinet ministers from provincial capitals averaged careers about a week shorter than the overall mean, while those from other towns and rural areas had longer careers by 2.29 to 4.47 months. Paradoxically, the further one was born from the seats of power, the more likely he was to serve a longer career. These results do not contradict the assumption that men born in cities had an

Table 5.8 Analysis of Variance of Total Months in the
Executive Elite by Politics, Title, Birthplace,
and Experience, 1824–1857

Grand Mean = 12.29		Unadjusted		Adjusted for Independents	
Variable + Category	N	Deviation	Eta	Deviation	Beta
Politics					
1 Radical	36	−7.85		−9.05	
2 Moderate	56	4.00		2.99	
3 Conservative	49	−0.17		1.56	
4 Santanista	14	4.78		5.85	
			0.29		0.31
Title					
1 Professional	63	0.07		−0.47	
2 Military	53	3.37		2.82	
3 None	39	−4.70		−3.08	
			0.19		0.14
Birthplace					
1 Mexico City	35	−4.92		−6.36	
2 Provincial Capital	46	−0.79		−0.27	
3 Other Town	28	2.76		2.29	
4 Rural	46	2.91		4.47	
			0.19		0.23
Experience as Governor					
0 No	109	0.12		0.25	
1 Yes	46	−0.29		−0.59	
			0.01		0.02
Experience as Legislator					
0 No	45	−3.12		−3.39	
1 Yes	110	1.32		1.43	
			0.12		0.14

Statistics: Source of Variation	Sum of Squares	DF	Mean Square	F	Significance of F
Main Effects	7144.266	10	714.427	3.023	0.002
Politics	3736.289	3	1245.430	5.269	0.002
Title	716.567	2	358.284	1.516	0.223
Birthplace	2041.037	3	680.346	2.878	0.038
Governor	19.596	1	19.596	0.083	0.774
Legislator	672.817	1	672.817	2.847	0.094

Table 5.8   (continued)

Statistics: Source of Variation	Sum of Squares	DF	Mean Square	F	Significance of F
Explained	7144.266	10	714.427	3.023	0.002
Residual	34035.669	144	236.359		
Total	41179.935	154	267.402		
Multiple R Squared = 0.173.					
Multiple R = 0.417.					

advantage in terms of schooling and social and political connections which made it easier for them to maintain power; those from
provincial capitals did tend to serve longer individual terms. Politicians from secondary towns and rural areas served only average
individual terms, but they were more likely to serve repeatedly and
lengthen their careers.

This result suggests an alternative explanation for the shorter
lengths of term and abbreviated careers of Mexico City natives.
Presidents and cabinet ministers born in Mexico City may have
enjoyed social connections which made access to high office easier,
but most of them served shorter terms and fewer months than their
colleagues from the provinces. Politicians born in provincial capitals served longer average terms, and those born in rural areas served
more months in power. This phenomenon may be explained by the
relative cost of obtaining their services. Having been born closer to
the locus of national power, the natives of Mexico City might be
expected to enjoy privileged access to education, wealth, and power.
Their transaction costs in accepting government posts were lower
in terms of the geographic distance they had to travel. The "psychic
costs" were lower as well, since they remained in close proximity to
friends and families. Social life in the national capital was apparently inhospitable to those without connections. Lucas Alamán,
himself a migrant to the capital, noted that entering Mexico City
society was difficult for strangers and that "the outsider who has
not been accepted into the domestic confidence of several families
finds nothing to do to pass the time but to ride around on horse-
back or to waste time in some café, if he is sufficiently restrained
not to look for another kind of distractions."[8]

The opportunity costs for natives of Mexico City were probably higher in terms of other alternatives in commerce and society. Natives of Mexico City might have been more willing to accept cabinet posts since their costs were lower in terms of distance, travel, and separation from friends and family than for someone who had to leave the provinces and work his way into the national capital's political hierarchy. Once in office, the relative costs of leaving power would be much greater for the native of a distant province, while the difference in wealth and social status between remaining in the cabinet and leaving it might well be meaningless to the Mexico City native. With other opportunities to pursue, those born in the commercial, social, and cultural capital of the nation might conclude that long service in the government was not worth the inconvenience. Perhaps the greater social advantages enjoyed by natives of Mexico City distracted them from government service, while the rural-born overcame disadvantages and showed a greater determination to maintain their powerful positions. This could explain why the politically and socially well-connected were more likely to serve short terms and brief careers. In any case, greater participation by Mexico's economic elite might have resulted in greater instability rather than more stable governments.

Political experience did not help either. When geographic background, training, and political faction are taken into account, experience as a state governor or a national legislator adds even less to explain total number of months in office than it does the individual lengths of terms.[9] No type of experience had much effect on the total number of months in the executive elite, nor is experience statistically significant at acceptable levels. Experience, or the lack of it, was less important in explaining instability than were the regional and political differences within the elite. This seems counterintuitive at first, since one might expect that more immediate sorts of practical training would be likely to have a greater effect in extending political careers than more remote indications of background. Birthplace, for example, is temporally and often geographically remote from the experience of governing, but the social connections for which birthplace is a proxy are profound. Political experience was less important as a source of stability than were variations in the origins and political programs of the men who held the top executive positions. Instability was not the result of individual characteristics. Instability was deeply rooted in Mexico's social and political landscapes.

Six

Social and Political

Landscapes

Nineteenth-century observers frequently noted the contradiction between liberal doctrine and the social realities
of Mexico after three hundred years of domination by
Spain. Conservatives denounced liberalism as an extraneous doctrine which brought inevitable degeneration to a stable society. They
blamed instability on liberals who had adopted foreign political
ideologies and imported exotic institutions which were out of touch
with Mexico's social and historical reality. Conservatives argued
that instability could be ended by establishing a political system
that conformed to the existing social reality. This required impos-
ing a strong executive, or better yet a monarchy, and a stratified,
hierarchical political system to stabilize and sustain the stratified,
hierarchical social structure.

Conservatives were not alone in noting the incompatibility of
existing Mexican society to liberal political ideals. Even avowed
liberals were daunted by the prospects of applying liberal doctrines
to Mexico. José María Luis Mora, one of the leading liberals of his
day, regarded the distance between liberal ideas and the social reality of Latin America as the principal cause for the instability that
followed independence. Mora observed that the new republics "have
not adopted of the representative system anything but its forms and
its exterior apparatus."[1] As a liberal, Mora concluded that his political ideals were not the source of the problem, but that drastic measures should be taken to transform society to make it consistent

with liberal politics. While conservatives wanted to adapt government to maintain Mexico's traditional class structure, liberals sought
to alter social relations to fit to republican institutions.

To speak of a single Mexican social structure is, of course,
overly general. Mexican society was not uniform, and social structures varied with geography. Over the last thirty years historians
have shown a great interest in regional variation in Mexico's social
structure, especially during the periods of rebellion and revolution
which began and ended the nineteenth century.[2] Several historians
have noted geographic variation in the origins of conservative and
liberal politicians and have suggested a relationship between regional
social structures and the roots of political factionalism. As long ago
as 1938, Henry Bamford Parkes put the relationship this way:

> The strength of the conservatives lay in the City of Mexico
> and in the central provinces, where Spanish rule had been most
> firmly established. Liberalism prevailed in the mountains of
> the South and in the northern territories—Zacatecas and Du-
> rango and San Luis Potosí—where property was more evenly
> divided, with fewer haciendas and a larger number of ranche-
> ros, and where Indian tribes were more militant.[3]

Parkes noted that the conservatives promoted centralized government which would continue Mexico City's domination of the
provinces, and that provincial liberals, mestizo caciques "who em-
bodied the will of the masses," used guerrilla warfare to fight central control. While historians have commonly noted the regional
divisions apparent in the struggles between centralists and federal-
ists and in the Wars of the Reform,[4] Parkes related the origins of
political struggles to differences in regional social structures.

These identifications between conservatives, the traditional elite,
and Mexico City on the one hand, and liberals, rancheros, and the
provinces on the other have been expanded by other historians. In
the 1960s François Chevalier compared the relative social equality
of the area north and west of Mexico City to the more stratified
society of the capital's immediately surrounding area.[5] David
Brading extended this hypothesis and elaborated upon it. He proposed the existence of two regions where distinct social structures
gave rise to competing liberal and conservative politicians: a central
conservative core and a "Liberal Crescent."

The conservative core surrounding Mexico City had been densely settled and socially stratified when the Spanish arrived in Mexico. The city itself was the administrative seat of the Aztec empire and became the center of government for the colony of New Spain. The hacienda dominated the rural areas of the central core, where estate owners restricted labor through debt peonage, and pressure for land limited the freedom of those independent Indian villages that remained. The conservative political climate of the central core could be traced through centuries of social stratification, centralization of power, and inequality in the distribution of land.

The conservative core was surrounded by what Brading called the "Liberal Crescent," consisting of "a vast arc of territory stretching from Guerrero, through Michoacán, Jalisco, part of Guanajuato, Zacatecas, and San Luis Potosí to Veracruz."[6] In this region settlement after the conquest had resulted in a greater degree of social equality and diversity in both the city and the countryside. Citing regional studies of the Bajío, certain districts of San Luis Potosí, and the Altos of Jalisco and Michoacán, Brading noted the existence of "a complex society, both urban and rural, in which various elements or strata found in liberalism the appropriate vehicle for the expression of their ambitions, aspirations and resentments." Rather than being dominated by large haciendas and Indian villages, the rural areas of the liberal crescent included substantial numbers of rancheros, "a broad middle segment composed of small proprietors and substantial tenant farmers."[7] In the cities which dotted the liberal crescent, petty merchants, muleteers, miners, and textile workers, as well as craftsmen and other small property owners, created an appropriate climate for the growth of liberalism.

Over the years Brading's lucid and carefully specified hypothesis has enjoyed wide acceptance as an explanation of the relationship between early republican politics and social structure, but the hypothesis (and Brading stressed that it was only a hypothesis) has not previously been tested systematically.[8] Relatively little of the local research has been undertaken,[9] but each historian who has helped develop the hypothesis has noted the prominent national politicians who fit the regional patterns. Parkes cited a single example, Juan Alvarez, who dominated the mountains to the south of Mexico City. Alvarez was a ranchero who "was proud of the fact that he plowed the land with his own hands."[10] Brading noted seven additional examples of liberals who came from the states of the liberal crescent: Santos Degollado, Melchor Ocampo, Pedro Ogazón, Manuel Doblado, Jesús González Ortega, Miguel Lerdo de Tejada, and Manuel Gutiérrez Zamora. These examples are suggestive, but only a systematic study of a broader political spectrum can determine overall patterns and adequately test the hypothesis.

An attempt to study the relationship between politics and society requires careful definition of underlying assumptions. One of these assumptions concerns the mechanism by which social structure would affect political philosophies and actions. Most research on social origins hypotheses in other areas of the world has tended to find that "the correlations between social background and policy preferences are remarkably weak and unpredictable."[11] Of course, there are individual cases where members of the elite deliberately and consciously expressed the interests of their social class or geographic region.[12] But it is unnecessary to find personal financial motives for each individual's political decisions. In fact, given the recent emphasis on the tendency of businessmen to diversify their investments, it may be considered unlikely that they represented the interests of a single sort of investment.[13] A more subtle version of this hypothesis would hold that favoritism for class or region results from habits of thought and the unconscious influence of past experience on outlook and reasoning.

Further assumptions are necessary to describe how such a survey might be carried out. Three definitions must be explicit: (1) which individuals to include, (2) how to identify their politics, and (3) how to connect them with the regions. The existing literature contains implicit answers to each.

With a single exception, all the politicians cited as examples by Parkes and Brading served as presidents of the republic or in the cabinet ministries.[14] Rather than selecting a few examples to support the hypothesis from among the scores of occupants of those political offices, it would seem reasonable to study everyone who held office as cabinet ministers or presidents during the period. The following tables include all cabinet ministers and presidents between 1824 and 1867 for whom the other data could be determined.

Political positions can be readily determined since these were, after all, prominent politicians. Most were well-known and their political positions were noted by their contemporaries and by successive generations of historians. Many took strong positions which made them controversial at the time, and these controversies account for the public clamor for changes in the ministries. Three principal political positions have been identified: radical, moderate, and conservative.[15]

But how to connect individuals with regions? Parkes never clarified the basis for his regional identifications. It is not obvious what Parkes meant when he wrote that the "strength" of the conservatives "lay" in the center or that liberalism "prevailed" in the peripheral southern mountains and northern states. He implied some fundamental link in addition to the military positions each army occupied in the War of the Reform, but just what was that connection? Here, Brading is more explicit, noting examples of "leading liberals who came from those states" and asking, "Was this regional division a mere accident, the product of military exigencies, or was it based upon differences in social structure?"[16]

The question of where one is "from" may be answered by place of birth, or where one "grows up." These are often, but not always, the same. Birthplace has several advantages as a variable. First, it is more precise. When a family has moved from the place of a child's birth, the child may have trouble saying where he is "from," but no such ambiguity exists with birthplace. Second, the question of where one grows up, or is educated, or has another formative experience, begins to move subtly from the question of family origins to the individual's place of socialization. These formative experiences and the socialization process should not be dismissed, but neither should the question of birthplace be confused with that of socialization.[17] Third, in the absence of some relationship between birthplace and local social structures, birthplaces would be randomly distributed. Certainly, place of birth is random from the point of view of the child who has no control over the location of his family at the time of his birth. Yet it is just this seeming randomness of location which makes place of birth an interesting variable. Unless there is some connection between the location of a family on the child's birth and regional variations in social structures, we would not expect to find any significant relationship between an individual's eventual political position and his place of birth. Birthplace has the advantage, then, of being at once unambiguous, unlikely to be

Table 6.1 Politicians Born in Brading's "Core" and "Crescent"

	"Conservative Core"	"Liberal Crescent"	Total
Liberals	32 (40%)	48 (60%)	80
	(49%)	(62%)	
Conservatives	33 (52%)	30 (48%)	63
	(51%)	(38%)	
Total	65	78	143

Statistics: Phi = 0.123. Chi-square = 2.179 with 1 DF. Probability = 0.140.
Notes: "Conservative Core" includes birthplaces in what are now the city of Mexico and the states of Hidalgo, Mexico, and Puebla. "Liberal Crescent" includes birthplaces in what are now the states of Guanajuato, Guerrero, Jalisco, Michoacán, San Luis Potosí, Veracruz, and Zacatecas. This table does not include Santanistas. Defining Santanistas as conservatives would give results even less statistically significant by increasing the number of conservatives born in the liberal crescent.
    Row percentages are to the right of each figure; column percentages are below. Some rows and columns may not total 100 percent due to rounding.
Sources: See Appendix A.

under the conscious control of the individual, and at the same time a difficult test for the hypothesis that regional variations in social structures were related to political differences.

    Comparison of the birthplaces of liberals and conservatives in table 6.1 provides results which do not confirm Brading's version of the hypothesis. Table 6.1 compares political affiliations of presidents and cabinet ministers born in Brading's "Conservative Core" and the "Liberal Crescent." Almost as many liberals as conservatives were born in the central region Brading specified as the conservative core. Only slightly more than half the presidents and cabinet ministers born in the core conservative areas actually became conservatives, while 49 percent became liberals. Even taking the conservatives as a group, the connection between conservatism and central Mexico is rather weak. Only a bit more than half (53 percent) the conservatives were born in the core conservative states, while nearly half (48 percent) were born in the surrounding states Brading specified as the cradle of liberalism. The connection between the "Liberal Crescent" and the birthplaces of liberals is stronger. Sixty-two percent of those elite members born in the crescent became liberals and accounted for 60 percent of the liberals born in the two regions. Overall, the relationship between politics and region as defined by this hypothesis is weak, and the difference in proportions between the two regions is not statistically significant at usual levels. Such a distribution could be expected to occur at random 14 percent of the time.

Parkes defined his regions differently and stressed the importance of overt social conflicts. For Parkes, liberalism was connected somehow to the northern states such as Zacatecas, Durango, and San Luis Potosí and to the South. Recent historiography allows us to consider the possibilities suggested by Parkes linking liberalism and social conflict in these regions.

In the North,[18] a distinct society was created by the variation in military, ecclesiastical, and economic structures. Relatively low population density and more abundant land and opportunities made it impossible to maintain the complex institutions and more rigid social hierarchy of the center. The higher incidence of property ownership and the small scale of frontier settlements gave northerners a greater incentive to volunteer for military service and made the military more responsive to community needs. The danger of attacks by Apaches and other migrating tribes required cooperation between large and small landowners for the preservation of society. Militia members in the North could see the direct benefits of their service and were less likely to be drafted into the regular army, given the distance from central Mexico.[19] In addition, independence weakened the control of the central government, the military, and the Church, making northern Mexico more "democratic, fluid, and dynamic than central Mexico."[20]

In the North, then, an abundance of land and the danger of attacks by Apaches and Comanches mitigated social conflict between large and small landowners. In the South, as in central Mexico, settled agricultural Indian communities had been directly integrated into the colonial social system and competed with creole society for scarce resources. In contrast to central Mexico, where the weight of colonial authority, the Church, and the military weighed heavily on Indian society, Indian villages in southern Mexico seem to have been better able to resist. In Oaxaca, Indian communities continued largely intact during the colonial period while retaining or expanding their lands. Profit was not obtained by direct control over Indian land or labor but was gained through commerce that required less interference in the daily lives of Indians living in villages and fewer resident Spaniards.[21] The Oaxacan environment of indirect rule and commercial profit produced many of the nineteenth century's more important liberal politicians, foremost among them Benito Juárez. Conflicts between Indian villages and the colonial government could be more extreme in southern Mexico than in the center of the country, and rebels there were more likely to deny the legitimacy of the central government.[22] Yet expansion of agriculture into the Pacific lowlands produced not only the liberal ranchero Juan Alvarez, but the conservative Nicolás Bravo. Perhaps the internal social conflicts in the South inclined politicians from that region to more extreme solutions.

These observations suggest that the far North and the South were more likely to produce liberals than was a more broadly defined central region. Table 6.2 presents a breakdown of elite birthplaces by region and distinguishes among Mexico City, the state of Veracruz, and the regions of central Mexico, the North, and the South. The resulting difference in proportions is highly significant in statistical terms, and the variations in proportions of politicians are consistent with the hypothesis. The central region was home to the majority of these elite politicians, whether radical, moderate, or conservative, but in significantly different proportions. Eighty-eight percent of the conservatives were born in the region of Mexico City, Veracruz, and the surrounding states. In contrast, liberals were more likely to be born into families in the peripheral areas of the North or the South. Only 68 percent of the moderates and 57 percent of the radicals were born relatively close to the viceregal, and later national, capital.

The state of Veracruz has enjoyed a reputation as a bastion of liberalism dating from Manuel Gutiérrez Zamora's administration and Benito Juárez's occupation of the port, but the state produced more conservatives than liberals. Narrowing the definition of the conservative core to Mexico City and the state of Veracruz produces a majority of conservative births in those areas. More than half of all future presidents and cabinet ministers from 1824 to 1867 who were born in Mexico City or the state of Veracruz grew up to be conservatives, while only about one-fifth of those born in North and South did so. A further 29 percent of those born in the viceregal capital became moderates, but the capital produced few radicals. The state of Veracruz was home to Antonio López de Santa

Table 6.2 Political Affiliation by Region of Birthplace

	Mexico City	State of Veracruz	Center	North	South	Total
Radicals	7 (13%)	8 (15%)	16 (29%)	16 (29%)	8 (15%)	55
	(14%)	(24%)	(25%)	(42%)	(53%)	
Moderates	14 (23%)	6 (10%)	21 (35%)	15 (25%)	4 (7%)	60
	(29%)	(18%)	(33%)	(39%)	(27%)	
Conservatives	28 (33%)	20 (24%)	26 (31%)	7 (8%)	3 (4%)	84
	(57%)	(59%)	(41%)	(18%)	(20%)	
Total	49	34	63	38	15	199

Statistics: Cramer's $V = 0.250$. Chi-square $= 24.787$ with 8 DF. Probability $= 0.0017$.
Notes: "Center" includes birthplaces in what are now the states of Guanajuato, Hidalgo, Jalisco, Mexico, Michoacán, Nayarít, Puebla, and Queretaro. "North" includes birthplaces in what are now the states of Aguascalientes, Coahuila, Chihuahua, Durango, Nuevo León, San Luis Potosí, Sonora, Tamaulipas, Zacatecas, and Texas. "South" includes birthplaces in the states of Campeche, Chiapas, Guerrero, and Oaxaca.
    Row percentages are to the right of each figure; column percentages are below. Some rows and columns may not total 100 percent due to rounding.
Sources: See Appendix A.

Anna, but only seven of the twenty conservatives born in Veracruz were closely identified with him. With the exception of Veracruz and Mexico City, the states in the central region produced politicians with diverse outlooks in roughly equal proportions. About one-third of each political faction came from the central states.

    Although the North and the South provided smaller numbers of elite politicians than did the center, the patterns in their regional distribution are generally consistent with the hypothesis. The social conditions of northern and southern Mexico apparently produced distinctive types of politicians. The more informal, egalitarian North produced proportionately more moderates and radicals than conservatives. Eighty-two percent of those born in the North became liberals; only 18 percent were inclined to conservatism. Roughly one-quarter of all moderates were born in the North, but very few came from southern families. Southern Mexico produced a preponderance of radical politicians, but relatively few political moderates or conservatives of national importance.

    These variations in the birthplaces of the national executive elite assume that a "region" is an area bounded by the political divisions between states. Yet within each state the social geography is likely to differ significantly with the features of the economic and political landscape. The variations observed between the national capital and the states around it hint that there might have been important differences between other cities and the surrounding countryside. Prominent and powerful families were more likely to reside in urban than in rural areas and more often in administrative centers than in less significant towns or villages. Mariano Otero observed that those with political power and social position in nineteenth-century Mexico were most likely to be residents of Mexico City or to a slightly lesser degree to reside in a state or provincial administrative center.[23] Even major landowners were more likely to maintain their principal residences in large population centers rather than on their haciendas in the countryside, leaving the rural areas to the workers and administrators.[24] These observations suggest that a child's birthplace may give a rough indication of his family's economic condition and political importance. The heirs of the national elite would be more likely to be born in Mexico City, and the offspring of provincial elites in their state capitals. Children born into small town and rural families might be expected to come from poorer families with fewer relatives in powerful positions.

The political struggles between the national capital and the provinces make up a frequent theme in the literature, and this general conflict may well have had its roots in the social conflict between national elites, provincial families, and the upwardly mobile. According to this hypothesis, liberals came from families without connections to the colonial administration or Church hierarchy. They were outsiders without easy access to administrative centers, important markets, or higher education. Their years of study and training in the capital were, in the words of Frank Safford, "a time of struggle and isolation" without family and friends to ease the way for them. Although they eventually attained social positions and political power commensurate with conservatives, the liberals started their careers in very different places and overcame greater obstacles which left the sons of the provinces with a desire to destroy the structures and institutions that had stifled them.[25]

While it would be difficult to confirm the emotional conditions, mental states, and motivations this hypothesis suggests for the liberal reformers of the period, some aspects of the hypothesis

Table 6.3   Political Affiliation by Location of Birthplace

	National Capital	Provincial Capitals	Other Urban	Rural	Total
Radicals	7 (13%)	17 (32%)	16 (30%)	13 (25%)	53
Moderates	14 (24%)	12 (20%)	21 (36%)	12 (20%)	59
Conservatives	28 (35%)	29 (36%)	17 (21%)	7 (9%)	81
Total	49	58	54	32	193

Statistics: Cramer's V = 0.210. Chi-square = 16.996 with 6 DF. Probability = 0.0093.
Notes: Some rows may not total 100 percent due to rounding.
Sources: See Appendix A.

can be explored empirically. The proposition that liberals were out-siders who grew up far from the "nodes of power" is consistent with the data in table 6.3. Conservatives were more likely than liberals to be born into families residing in administrative centers. More than two-thirds of the Mexican conservative elite were born in either Mexico City or a provincial capital. Fewer than half of the radicals and moderate liberals were born in cities with either na-tional or provincial administrations.

Table 6.3 also indicates that there was a statistically significant division among radicals, moderates, and conservatives on the basis of rural or urban birthplaces. Although the majority of each faction were born into urban families, liberals were roughly twice as likely as conservatives to be born in the countryside. The percentage of rural births varied from 25 percent for radicals and 20 percent for moderates to only 9 percent for conservatives. The Mexican politi-cal elite was overwhelmingly urban, and most shared similar aspi-rations about the future of the countryside. Though a few radicals argued for redistribution of wealth to benefit the rural lower class, many liberals as well as conservatives aspired to own haciendas, and the liberal theory of the benefits of small landownership got little support as a program.[26] Nevertheless, liberals, and especially radi-cal liberals, were more likely than conservatives to have family roots in the countryside.[27]

Regional interpretations of political conflict in Mexico have a long lineage. Historians typically agree that conservative strength lay in the conservative core of Mexico City and Puebla and that liberalism was stronger in a crescent that arced around this region from Veracruz northwest to Zacatecas and south to Guerrero. Until now, the evidence to support this hypothesis has been largely anecdotal and unsystematic. The analysis presented here modifies and extends this hypothesis. While the traditionally conservative capital, seat of both the Aztec empire and colonial New Spain, did produce a preponderance of conservative politicians, it also gave birth to a fair number of moderate and even a handful of radical politicians. The central region as a whole (including the liberal crescent) was ethnically and socially complex and produced a diverse group of politicians distributed across the political spectrum. In both the North and the South, social structure seems to have been less complex and the relationship between politics and social divisions more direct. In the North, an abundance of land and the danger of attacks by migrating tribes external to society may have required cooperation between large and small property owners for the preservation of society. This social environment produced liberals but few conservatives. In the South, conflicts between Indian villages and creole haciendas were internal to society. The antagonistic social structure of the South produced a preponderance of radicals but proportionately fewer moderates or conservatives. The majority of each faction were born to families residing in major cities and towns, but in the roots of their families there were significant differences between factions. Radicals and moderate liberals were roughly twice as likely to come from families who lived in the countryside at the time they were born. Conservatives were most frequently born to families residing in administrative centers with their easier access to the wealthy and the powerful. Very few conservatives came from families with their roots in the countryside, and very few radicals were natives of Mexico City. These results tend to confirm the hypothesis that geographic variations in the origins of the national political elite reflected social distinctions and class relations.

Regional variation in the origins of political groups suggests a connection between social structure and political ideology, but the identification is not complete. The traditionally conservative capital produced more than the expected number of conservative leaders, but Mexico City also produced a large number of moderate liberals and even a small number of radicals. The relationship between a regional social structure and the social origins of politicians from that region is problematic, given the potential ecological fallacy. That is, social structures and the birthplaces of politicians may have similar geographic distributions without any actual correlation between specific individuals and classes. Even if conservatives were more likely to be born into the area of high elite concentration in Mexico City, any verifiable connection between those individuals and that class remains to be proven. The regional origins of political ideology are strong and statistically significant, but region is only an imperfect approximation of social class and status.

Seven

Conditions and

Convictions

The linkage between political positions and social divisions can be measured more precisely by studying the relationship between politicians and social stratification in the national capital. The 1848 census of Mexico City provides the opportunity to examine the social variation among the politically active members of the elite.[1] Of approximately two hundred individuals who held office as president or cabinet minister between Independence and the Wars of the Reform and French Intervention, fifty-two were listed in the census.[2] A few examples will illustrate the possibilities of linking conventional political information to evidence from the census.[3]

José María Jáuregui, a fifty-three-year-old native of Veracruz, acted as minister of justice for a few weeks during the chaotic days during the U.S. invasion of Mexico in 1847. Little is known about his political opinions. Either he was fairly modest or the census taker was only perfunctory, for his occupation is listed as merely "employee." Jáuregui and his twenty-year-old wife were childless and had no domestic servants living in the household. They shared a modest apartment, the same three rooms Jáuregui had occupied for the last nine years in a house owned by the Hospital de Jesús, to which they paid 8 pesos a month in rent.

Juan Pablo Anaya, born in Lagos, Jalisco, in 1785, joined the insurgents when Hidalgo arrived in Guadalajara in November 1810, but he was involved in little combat. Anaya seconded the Plan of

Iguala in 1821, was raised to the rank of general de brigada in 1823, and served briefly as minister of war in 1833. By 1848 he was an elderly military officer and political moderate at the end of his career. He and his wife had lived alone for almost a year at Monte Pio #1, which they rented from a private landlord, Don Mariano P. Castro, for 15 pesos per month.

Miguel María Arrioja, born in the city of Puebla in 1807, would later serve as minister of foreign relations for a month in 1855 during Juan Alvarez's administration. Arrioja would make his reputation as a radical. In 1848 he was employed in the government and living at Santa Brígida y Letrán #1 with his wife, a daughter, and three sons, but no servants. The family had occupied the house for about five years, paying a rather substantial 90 pesos a month in rent to the convent of Santa Brígida.

Juan Rondero was a native of Puebla. A political moderate, Rondero was a prosperous merchant who served half a year as minister of hacienda in 1847. He lived in a house he owned, valued at 14,000 pesos, along with his wife, five children, two employees, and ten household servants. The house sheltered not only Rondero's large immediate family and his employees, but a number of others. Rondero was not so prosperous that he was averse to the additional income to be gained by renting portions of the house for a total of 30 pesos per month.

A prominent lawyer and political radical born in Orizaba, Veracruz, in 1803, José Bernardo Couto received his law degree at the Colegio de San Ildefonso in Mexico City. He later represented his home state many times in the national legislature and was appointed to the post of minister of justice in 1845. By 1848 Couto had been living for seven years in a large house at Acequia #7 with his wife and four children. Couto was apparently quite well-off. The family was attended by fourteen servants, and in an age when 90 percent of the city's elite rented their residences, Couto owned his own home, which was valued at $22,500.

Luis Gonzaga Cuevas was known as a political conservative with considerable experience in government. Born in Lerma in the state of Mexico in 1800, he also received his law degree from the Colegio de San Ildefonso in Mexico City. He made a profession of government service; by 1848 he already had served seven terms as minister of foreign relations and as minister of justice. He would later serve as minister of foreign relations for Félix Zuloaga and the conservatives during the War of the Reform. In addition to his government posts, Cuevas managed his investments; his occupation is listed in the census as "propietario." He lived with his wife and three young children at Montealegre #9 along with fifteen servants and two children of servants. The family enjoyed the attentions of a doorman, a housekeeper, a cook, a coachman, a footman, and numerous specialized maids. Despite the evident luxury of abundant household servants and his profession as a property owner, Cuevas did not own the building in which he lived. It belonged to a Don José María Cuevas, almost certainly a close relative, to whom he paid only 60 pesos per month in rent.

These examples suggest both the wealth of information that can be gleaned from the census and the complexity of any relationship between social conditions and political convictions. There was considerable variation between these individuals in their political positions, in the size and composition of their households, in the numbers of servants they employed, in their length of residence and political service, in their regional origins, and in the value and ownership of their dwellings. Studied together, these variables can provide a clearer understanding of the relationship between society and politics in mid-nineteenth-century Mexico.

The size of a household is generally a good indication of the family's social status. Historians and sociologists who have studied the family have found a remarkable degree of consistency in the size of the average household over the last several centuries. From England to Latin America the mean household size has remained fairly constant at about five, while varying with social class and economic means. The more prosperous have generally had larger households, the lower classes have had smaller households.[4] By this standard, most of the households of the mid-nineteenth-century political elite were large. Of the forty-three politicians whose households were enumerated in the census, more than 80 percent had six or more members, and more than half had nine or more people living under the same roof. At the same time, there was considerable variation among this political elite; households ranged in size from two to more than twenty (see table 7.1).

An anecdotal approach can suggest possibilities but quickly becomes bogged down in the fascinating facets of particular cases;

Table 7.1 Frequency Distribution of Household Sizes for
National Political Elite, Mexico City, 1848

Household Size	Frequency	Percentage	Cumulative Percentage
2−5	7	16.2	16.2
6−8	11	25.6	41.9
9−11	11	25.6	67.4
12−17	8	18.7	86.0
18−23	6	14.0	100.0

Statistics: Mean = 10.4. Median = 10.0. Mode = 7.0. SD = 5.4. Minimum = 2.0. Maximum = 23.0. N = 43.
Sources: Calculated from data in Padrón Municipalidad de México (1848), Archivo del Antiguo Ayuntamiento (Mexico City), v. 3408–3409. Appendix B provides a list of individuals included in this table, their classifications, and locations in the padrón.

the examples cited earlier are only six of several dozen possibilities. Clearly, a multivariate statistical analysis is in order to distinguish among the effects of the different variables and to attempt to describe the essential structure beneath the delicate ornamentation of the individual experiences and the complex interrelationships between multiple variables. For example, if we use household size as a proxy for social class, we would still expect the household to vary not only according to social status, wealth, or political philosophy, but with a number of other variables, such as age and marital status, which reflect the stage in the life cycle of the head of household. We would not want to confuse the effects of these other factors with those bearing directly on the question of social stratification and political ideas. For example, middle-aged married couples will usually have larger households on average than single young men or elderly widowers. We would expect age and marital status to be independent of social class and politics. In the same way, those prominent politicians who achieved a greater degree of success might be expected to have larger households than those with similar ideas who were not as successful in holding high office.

Such complications call for an approach which can separate the effects of the different variables. Analysis of covariance is a statistical technique that compares the effects of independent categorical divisions (called "factors") of a group on a continuous depen-

Table 7.2   Analysis of Covariance of Household Size by Politics, Political Endurance, and Marital Status (with age of tenant and years in residence held constant)

Grand Mean = 9.97

Variable + Category	N	Unadjusted		Adjusted for Independents + Covariates	
		Deviation	Eta	Deviation	Beta
Politics					
0 Unknown	6	1.53		1.18	
1 Radical	6	− 3.64		− 2.59	
2 Moderate	9	0.36		− 0.26	
3 Conservative	17	0.56		0.64	
			0.32		0.24
Political Endurance					
0 Up to 3 months	12	− 1.47		− 2.62	
1 4 to 11	13	− 0.05		− 0.37	
2 12 or more	13	1.41		2.79	
			0.23		0.44
Marital Status					
1 Single	8	− 2.47		− 4.18	
2 Married	25	0.95		1.51	
3 Widowed	5	− 0.77		− 0.87	
			0.28		0.46

Statistics: Source of Variation	Sum of Squares	DF	Mean Square	F	Significance of F
Covariates	17.264	2	8.632	0.366	0.696
Age	4.446	1	4.446	0.189	0.667
Years	16.268	1	16.268	0.691	0.413
Main Effects	290.210	7	41.459	1.760	0.135
Politics	46.921	3	15.640	0.664	0.581
Endurance	124.241	2	62.120	2.637	0.089
Marital Status	114.264	2	57.132	2.426	0.107
Explained	307.474	9	34.164	1.450	0.215
Residual	659.499	28	23.554		
Total	966.974	37	26.134		

Multiple R squared = 0.318.
Multiple R   = 0.564.
Sources: See Appendix B.

dent variable measured at the interval level (in this case, household size). At the same time, analysis of covariance adjusts for continuous variables (called covariates). This provides a correction for variables that are peripheral to this study: the age of the tenant and the number of years the family has occupied the dwelling. In other words, by distinguishing among the effects of the factors and covariates, analysis of covariance can determine whether conservatives, moderates, or radical liberals tended to have households of distinctly different sizes without regard to their ages, marital status, political durability, or length of residence.[5]

Table 7.2 displays the results of this analysis of covariance in multiple classification analysis format, permitting the comparison of means of subgroups as deviations from the grand mean for all groups, 9.97 members per household. The results show both unadjusted and adjusted deviations. The column labeled Unadjusted Deviation at the center of the table shows variations in group means before considering the effects of the covariates and other independent variables. Deviations adjusted for independent variables and covariates appear in the column at the right side of the table. The adjusted figures show variation in the group means after the effects of the other factors and covariates are taken into account; they avoid confusing the effects of multiple variables. For the independent variables studied in this table, the adjusted deviations refine the size of the deviations but do not change the relative positions of the groups.

These results confirm the speculation that household size varied with politics, success, and marital status. Single men tended to have substantially smaller households with more than four fewer residents than the overall average. Married men averaged households slightly larger than the grand mean, while widowers tended to have slightly smaller households.

The factor political endurance divides the renters into three groups of nearly equal size depending on the total number of months during his political career that each renter occupied a ministry or the presidency. The ability to maintain a long political career at the cabinet level is linked to socioeconomic status, as indicated by family size. Those who held a prominent position for a total of twelve months or more had an average of nearly three additional members resident in their households. Those with relatively average careers (totaling from four to eleven months in office) fall very close to the mean household size. The least prominent or enduring politicians averaged nearly three fewer persons than the mean and more than five fewer residents than the householders of the most politically prominent. These results show a positive correlation between political endurance and household size; those presidents and cabinet ministers who served the longest terms tended to have the largest households.

Radicals, moderates, and conservatives were all members of a social elite with households larger than the rest of the population, but the average size of their households varied between groups. After taking into account the effects of these other variables, there is some evidence that political convictions varied with social status. Moderates averaged households only slightly smaller than the mean for the elite as a whole, while conservatives tended to have slightly larger households. Both moderates and conservatives averaged households of about ten members, while radicals averaged considerably smaller households of between seven and eight residents. This places the radicals much closer to the average of the population as a whole. The variation between the mean household sizes of the political elite is consistent with the thesis that politics varied with social status. Radicals were likely to be less prosperous than moderates or conservatives.

The correlation between politics and household size raises other important questions. Those whose political positions could not be readily determined averaged the largest households, an observation that is difficult to explain. Part of the anomaly may result from the inadequacy of household size as a proxy for social status. Since households were composed of both family members and servants, the aggregate number of persons housed under a single roof may confound indications of social status with other conditions and preferences. A larger household might indicate only a desire to gather more family members under the same roof, or it may indicate the necessity of crowding more of the family together to save on housing costs. On the one hand, a large household may indicate that the family enjoyed the services of many household servants. On the other, a large household might require that housekeeping chores be carried out by numerous family members working at home, a potentially degrading inconvenience in an elite society that devalues

Table 7.3   Frequency Distribution of Household Servants for
National Political Elite, Mexico City, 1848

Number of Household Servants	Frequency	Percentage	Cumulative Percentage
0	3	7.0	7.0
1–2	11	25.6	32.6
3	10	23.3	55.9
4–6	13	30.2	86.1
7–15	6	13.9	100.0

Statistics: Mean = 4.1. Median = 3.0. Mode = 3.0. SD = 3.4. Minimum = 0.0. Maximum = 15.0. N = 43.
Sources: See Appendix B.

manual labor. The number of servants in the household might be a better indication of wealth and social position.

Silvia Arrom has suggested that the number of live-in servants is "perhaps the best single indicator of status in nineteenth-century Mexico."[6] From her analysis of the 1848 census, Arrom concluded that the upper class regularly employed at least three live-in servants in each household. This upper class may have constituted as much as 4 percent of the capital's population and included the wealthy nobles, miners, and merchants, and the top levels of the governmental, ecclesiastical, and military bureaucracies. The next 18 percent she described as intellectuals, clerks, professionals, modestly prosperous businessmen, lower clergy, and the middle ranks of the military, as well as the most prosperous artisans and small shopkeepers, who were still part of the *gente decente*. Although not designated "middle class" by their contemporaries, they lived quite comfortably and enjoyed the services of one or two live-in servants.

The data in table 7.3 show that the households of the political elite varied considerably in the number of domestics they employed. Very few had no live-in servants. Roughly one-quarter had only one or two household servants. The rest of the political elite, more than two-thirds of the total, maintained conspicuously upper-class households with three or more servants. This would place most elite politicians among the top 4 percent of the population of Mexico City. Since the national capital was the center of wealth and privilege in Mexico, this would probably mean that most of the

Table 7.4   Analysis of Covariance of Number of Domestic Servants by Politics, Political Endurance, and Marital Status (with age of tenant, years in residence, and family size held constant)

Grand Mean = 3.71

Variable + Category	N	Unadjusted		Adjusted for Independents + Covariates	
		Deviation	Eta	Deviation	Beta
Politics					
0 Unknown	6	−0.21		−1.27	
1 Radical	6	−2.71		−2.32	
2 Moderate	9	0.85		−0.13	
3 Conservative	17	0.58		1.33	
			0.43		0.48
Political Endurance					
0 Up to 3 months	12	−1.38		−1.03	
1 4 to 11	13	−0.10		−0.84	
2 12 or more	13	1.37		1.79	
			0.39		0.45
Marital Status					
1 Single	8	−1.46		−1.42	
2 Married	25	0.41		0.59	
3 Widowed	5	0.29		−0.68	
			0.27		0.30

Statistics: Source of Variation	Sum of Squares	DF	Mean Square	F	Significance of F
Covariates	39.629	3	13.210	2.282	0.102
Age	10.257	1	10.257	1.772	0.194
Years	2.297	1	2.297	0.397	0.534
Family	30.244	1	30.244	5.224	0.030
Main Effects	111.872	7	15.982	2.761	0.027
Politics	45.988	3	15.329	2.648	0.069
Endurance	46.105	2	23.052	3.982	0.031
Marital Status	15.312	2	7.656	1.322	0.283
Explained	151.502	10	15.150	2.617	0.023
Residual	156.314	27	5.789		
Total	307.816	37	8.319		

Multiple R squared = 0.492.
Multiple R   = 0.702.
Sources: See Appendix B.

political elite were part of an even smaller and distinctly prosperous percentage of the Mexican population as a whole. Half of these politicians were probably merely wealthy, enjoying the attentions of between three and six servants. The most affluent 14 percent lived extravagantly in households served by seven or more domestics. At the top end of the scale, the most opulent households had a dozen or more housekeepers, cooks, scullions, chambermaids, nursemaids, doormen, coachmen, footmen, valets, and others to attend to their comfort. These figures indicate considerable social stratification within the political elite. While most of these politicians were very well-off, a substantial portion lived notably less luxurious lives. Even among those able to hire several specialized servants, there was substantial variation.

Table 7.4 addresses the question of whether the political factions varied in average numbers of household servants. As before, the table includes covariates and factors to account for other sources of variation due to age, years in residence, marital status, and political durability. This table adds family size as a covariate so that the average numbers of servants in each group will not be affected by variations in the size of families. The grand mean for the thirty-eight cases without missing data is 3.7 servants per household. The numbers again indicate greater prosperity for the politically durable and the married. The elite politicians who held office for a year or more in their careers had nearly 50 percent more servants in their homes than the average. Single men averaged fewer servants than either widowers or married men.

Once again, when these other factors are taken into account, the political factions vary in social status. Conservatives had more servants per household. At a mean of five, the average number of servants in conservative households is 36 percent higher than the grand mean, placing the conservatives well into that tiny fraction of the total population that was the upper class. Moderates tended to have an average number of domestics not much smaller than the grand mean, placing them toward the lower end of the upper 4 percent of the population. Those whose politics could not be determined and the radicals employed the fewest servants. Radicals had 62 percent fewer domestics than the grand mean, placing them in the social strata where one to two household servants were common. Although they were still part of the *gente decente*, the radicals

Table 7.5   Political Factions by Ownership of Residence

	Owner-Occupied	Rented from Private Landlord	Rented from Church	Total
Unknown	2 (20%)	3 (30%)	5 (50%)	10
	(33%)	(21%)	(16%)	
Radical	1 (11%)	2 (22%)	6 (67%)	9
	(17%)	(14%)	(19%)	
Moderate	1 (10%)	1 (10%)	8 (80%)	10
	(17%)	(7%)	(25%)	
Conservative	2 (9%)	8 (35%)	13 (56%)	23
	(33%)	(57%)	(41%)	
Total	6 (11.5%)	14 (26.9%)	32 (61.5%)	52

Notes: Row percentages are to the right of each figure; column percentages are below.
Sources: See Appendix B.

lived in conditions less lofty than the economic and social strata of the conservatives.

The census data permit yet another attempt to test the relationship between social and political divisions. In mid-nineteenth-century Mexico City, few families, even among the social and political elite, owned their own homes. Of the former or soon-to-be presidents and cabinet ministers resident in the city in January 1848, only about 12 percent (six of fifty-two) owned their residences.[7] Given the infrequency of ownership, the majority rented. Two-thirds of the total rented from the Church, or, more precisely, from various convents, monasteries, hospitals, schools, parishes, chapels, churches, and pious funds. The remaining quarter rented from private landlords. The relationship between landlord type and political categories is not strong, but the direction of the relationship is intriguing. Liberals, who supported proposals to require the Church to sell its property to private individuals, were more likely to rent from the Church than were conservatives, who defended the Church from liberalism. A large majority of the liberals (80 percent of the moderates and 67 percent of the radicals) paid rent to ecclesiastical corporations. In contrast, only a little more than half of the conservatives rented from the Church, while the other half rented from private owners or owned their own homes (see table 7.5).

Rent, like the other indicators of social status, varied considerably within the elite. Table 7.6 indicates that most of the rents paid by the national political elite fell into the range between $25 and $75 monthly. Since nearly 90 percent of the elite rented rather than owned their homes, we would expect these variations in rent to be positively correlated with status; the greater a family's wealth, the more they would spend on housing to enjoy the comforts of money, to entertain friends, and to impress acquaintances. Rents paid by the political elite in 1848 varied from a low of $7 per month paid by Luis Arroyo (a thirty-year-old unmarried conservative) to a high of $125 per month paid by Ignacio Trigueros (a forty-four-year-old married conservative). Certainly, other factors enter into the equation besides income: family size, years of residence, age of housing, location, and taste, for example. Of these variables, most can be accounted for statistically, but location does not seem to have had a significant impact on the rental cost of housing among the elite. Nearly all of the political elite (88.5 percent) lived in the area within a few blocks of the Zocalo, and the rents of those who lived on the capital's fringes were not significantly lower than the average.[8]

The literature from the period suggests an additional variable which would influence the rent paid for a house in Mexico City. Houses there were expensive and hard for outsiders to find. Even during the boom years at the end of the eighteenth century, little new housing was constructed. There is little reason to believe that much improvement in the supply of housing took place after independence, given the deleterious effects of instability and war which not only hampered the economy but brought more migrants to the city. Shortages of housing were common in nineteenth-century Mexico.[9]

Preferential renting at below-market rates may have been one way families helped to mitigate these circumstances. The experiences of one of Mexico City's most famous new residents illustrate the problems of new arrivals in the city even for those with substantial financial resources. Frances Calderón de la Barca, the wife of the first Spanish ambassador to Mexico, arrived in late 1839 to find that rents for houses in the city were "extremely high," adding that in the capital there was "nothing tolerable to be had under two

Table 7.6   Frequency Distribution of Monthly Rents Paid by
National Political Elite, Mexico City, 1848

Amount of Monthly Rent (pesos)	Frequency	Percentage	Cumulative Percentage
7–25	7	15.2	15.2
26–40	11	23.9	39.1
41–50	11	23.9	63.0
51–75	11	23.9	86.9
76–125	6	13.0	99.9

Statistics: Mean = 48.1. Median = 46.0. Mode = 60.0. SD = 25.3. Minimum = 7.0.
Maximum = 125.0. N = 46.
Sources: See Appendix B.

thousand five hundred dollars per annum, unfurnished."[10] This is a
sum roughly twice the highest rent paid by a member of the political elite in 1848, and one suspects that the landlords of Mexico City
were suggesting rents far beyond the normal, assuming the new
ambassador would pay. Securing a residence required not only ap-
peasing the owner, but, at times, the previous tenant as well. Among
other expenses, Madam Calderón de la Barca noted "the extraordinary custom of paying a sum called *traspaso*, sometimes to the
amount of fourteen thousand dollars, taking your chance of having
the money repaid you by the next person who takes the house."
After weeks of looking for a suitable home, she was ready to explain the problems she faced, noting in her journal, "As to prices, I
conclude we pay for being foreigners and diplomates."

The Calderóns' search for a suitable residence might not have
been unique. Internal migrants as well as international travelers had
imperfect knowledge of the housing market in Mexico City, and
migrants to the capital from the Mexican provinces faced an additional obstacle, a steep increase in the amount they would need to
spend on housing. Once again, this fact did not escape the observation of Fanny Calderón. Sometime later, while on a tour of the
provinces, she noticed that the rents were much lower outside Mexico City. From the capital of the state of Michoacán, she wrote,
"Living and house-rent is so cheap here, that a family who could
barely exist upon their means in Mexico, may enjoy every luxury in
Valladolid."[11] The natives of Mexico City and the capital's long-

term residents, those with kin and other social connections, may well have had an advantage through increased knowledge of the housing market and through preferential treatment by landlords. The market may have worked against outsiders.[12]

These variables are examined in table 7.7, which displays mean house rents for social and political groups, controlling for the effects of the covariates age, years in residence, family size, and numbers of domestic servants. The factors which affected rents include the origin of the head of household. The results indicate that natives of Mexico City did enjoy a comparative advantage in the national capital's housing market. Elite politicians with provincial origins tended to pay $54 per month in rent, while those born in the capital paid only about $34, a difference amounting to about 50 percent for provincial politicians in otherwise equal social circumstances. Those who rented from the Church also paid a premium amounting to about 50 percent; those who paid rents to private landlords average $33, while those renting from the Church paid a mean of $53 per month. Other things being equal, the best housing deals in the national capital were enjoyed by natives of the city who rented from private individuals rather than the Church.

The widest variations in house rent are associated with variations in politics. Moderates and conservatives paid rents that were nearly equivalent and roughly 15 percent less than the average for all groups. Only about a peso and a half per month separated the average rents of these two groups, a difference equivalent to about 3 percent of the average monthly rent. This similarity in social condition between the conservatives and the moderate liberals stands in contrast to the social distance between them and the more extreme liberals. The radicals paid rents considerably higher by more than $17 per month, a sum 37 percent higher than the mean. The difference is especially pronounced between the rents of the radicals and the rest; with an average monthly house rent of $62.9, radicals paid 56 percent more than the average paid by conservatives ($40.2), and 63 percent more than the average rent paid by moderates ($38.7). Given that radicals tended to have smaller households and fewer servants than the other two groups, it seems likely that the higher rents radicals paid took a larger bite out of household budgets than the relatively lower amounts paid by moderates and conservatives. Those who were most determined to alter the distribution of prop-

Table 7.7   Analysis of Covariance of Rent by Politics, Political Endurance, Regional Origin, and Owner of Dwelling (with age of tenant, years in residence, family size, and servants held constant)

Grand Mean = 45.79

Variable + Category	N	Unadjusted Deviation	Eta	Adjusted for Independents + Covariates Deviation	Beta
Politics					
0 Unknown	6	4.54		9.06	
1 Radical	6	0.54		17.13	
2 Moderate	9	0.65		−7.04	
3 Conservative	17	−2.14		−5.52	
			0.11		0.42
Political Endurance					
0 Up to 3 months	12	−8.54		−12.84	
1 4 to 11	13	3.36		10.74	
2 12 or more	13	4.52		1.11	
			0.26		0.43
Regional Origin					
1 Mexico City	16	−7.66		−11.85	
2 Provincial	22	5.57		8.62	
			0.30		0.46
Owner of Dwelling					
1 Private	14	−7.00		−12.96	
2 Church	24	4.09		7.56	
			0.24		0.45

Statistics:

Source of Variation	Sum of Squares	DF	Mean Square	F	Significance of F
Covariates	2596.701	4	649.175	1.967	0.129
Age	0.726	1	0.726	0.002	0.963
Years	10.925	1	10.925	0.033	0.857
Family	783.017	1	783.017	2.373	0.136
Servants	975.197	1	975.197	2.955	0.098
Main Effects	7462.882	7	1066.126	3.230	0.013
Politics	1986.113	3	662.038	2.006	0.138
Endurance	2352.044	2	1176.022	3.563	0.043
Native	3179.627	1	3179.627	9.634	0.005
Owner	2576.399	1	2576.399	7.807	0.010
Explained	10059.584	11	914.508	2.771	0.016
Residual	8580.732	26	330.028		

Table 7.7   (continued)

Statistics: Source of Variation	Sum of Squares	DF	Mean Square	F	Significance of F
Total	18640.316	37	503.792		
Multiple R squared = 0.540.					
Multiple R = 0.735.					
Sources: See Appendix B.					

erty in Mexico were those whose personal situations demonstrated to them the existence of a link between the conservative policies and the economic advantages of their political opponents.

These articulations between social strata and political divisions in nineteenth-century Mexico have long been the subject of speculation, but seldom the object of investigation. Previously, little direct evidence has been brought to bear on the questions raised by generations of historians who have suggested links between social conditions and political convictions. Earlier investigations have examined two proxies for social class—occupation and regional origins. Of these, occupation is the more superficial. The political factions of postindependence Mexico were not readily distinguishable by the professions of their leaders; most of the liberals as well as the conservatives tended to be lawyers or military officers.

Differences in regional origins may have been more significant. Historians have traditionally linked conservatives to the economic and social elite resident in Mexico City. The hypothetical relationship between the social stratification of the capital and the political fissures evident in the political conflict of the time has been marred by a potential ecological fallacy. The traditional capital was, in fact, the birthplace of a preponderance of conservative politicians, and Mexico City was home to a disproportionately large number of colonial New Spain's and republican Mexico's wealthy and powerful families. Yet this essential connection between the social and the political elites has not been demonstrated before. Lacking crucial evidence, the arguments linking social strata to political factions have been only speculation, and the hypothesis of a connection between region and politics has been subject to the appropriate logical qualification that the ecological fallacy might apply. There

was no systematic evidence linking conservative politics to the economic elite.

The evidence examined here is subject to a number of limitations and qualifications. Roughly two hundred men dominated the
executive offices of the national government between independence
and the Wars of the Reform and French Intervention. This group
was not selected randomly; it is a stratified sample, consisting of
only elite executives. It may be that different results might apply if a
political elite were studied on the basis of legislative, local government, or other experience. Roughly one-quarter of the national
executive elite were residents of the national capital in 1848. In some
ways, the census data are a fortuitous sample; some of the elite had
died before 1848, others were living elsewhere, and several residents were not adequately enumerated by the census taker. Enough
crucial data were missing to reduce the number of cases used in the
analyses of variance from fifty-two to thirty-eight. Despite these
limitations, these three dozen individuals are nearly 20 percent of
the men who served as presidents or cabinet ministers during the
period.

The study is also limited geographically. In a country as varied
as Mexico, it may well be that different patterns applied in other
regions. The relationship between social conditions and political
convictions in the provinces would certainly be worth investigat-
ing, but in many ways a study of the elite in Mexico City has its
advantages. The national capital drew ambitious politicians from
the outlying states and may be more representative of the nation as
a whole than any other single city or state. At the same time, there
is no reason to slip back into the assumption that the individuals
who migrated from a particular state were representative of any
particular class there.

Nor can such a study be expected to explain every individual
case that could arise. Radicals in general may have come from a
lower social strata, and they may have disproportionately felt the
pressures of an expensive and arbitrary housing market in the national capital, but one of the examples cited earlier conspicuously
contradicts this generalization. José Bernardo Couto was a radical
but he lived well, served by fourteen domestics in an expensive
house that he owned rather than rented. Thus, wealthy radicals
certainly existed, but they were not as common as prosperous moderates and plutocratic conservatives. The condition of any individ-

ual is not a refutation of the general trends and multivariate analysis presented here. Statistical anomalies will always exist, and the idiosyncratic example does not invalidate the generalization.

This research is also limited in its ability to examine the family beyond the immediate household. Much of the speculation here, suggesting that many prosperous families paid what seem to be unreasonably low rents as a result of social connections, can be subject to empirical verification. Investigation of the family or business relationships between landlords and tenants might well require a modification of these hypotheses, but evidence from other historical and anthropological studies suggests that the hypothesis is at least reasonable. Kinship can substantially affect access to the housing market and the location of residences.

Subject to these qualifications and limitations, the data examined here lead to the conclusion that the social differences were politically significant. The political factions of mid-nineteenth-century Mexico did vary in wealth and social position. The national political elite was drawn from middle to upper classes, placing its members among the top 20 percent or so of the Mexican population. Within this stratum, the factions occupied different positions in that hierarchy. Political radicals occupied the lower rungs of the social elite; they were more likely to have smaller households and fewer servants than the upper class. Conservatives held the uppermost social positions with the largest households and greatest profusion of household servants. Moderates tended to occupy the intermediate social space; they were neither so opulent and pampered as the conservatives, nor as unpretentious and prosaic as the radicals.

On the basis of these variables, the social hierarchy seems clear and direct, but the rents these families paid for housing do not correspond directly to their social positions. Moderates and conservatives tended to have larger households and more servants, but they paid lower monthly rents than the radicals. Ownership also had a significant impact on house rent. The Church tended to charge rents that were substantially higher, in equal circumstances, than the rents charged by private landlords. Part of this differential may be due not to the Church's deviation from prevailing market rates, but to family members granting their relatives preferential access to housing. In addition, anecdotal evidence suggests that prevailing rents were probably higher in general in the capital than in the provinces. According to a contemporary observation, an income that permitted a life of luxury in the provinces was not sufficient in Mexico City. Together, these circumstances put additional pressure on the household budgets of those outsiders who migrated from the provinces to take up positions in the national political elite. Family connections and long-term residence probably meant that the natives of the city got the best deals. This argument suggests another intriguing hypothesis: the Church may not have been as great an obstacle to the operation of market forces in the capital as the actions and preferences of private landlords. If private landlords tended to discriminate by renting at discount rates to kin and business associates, the rents charged by the Church might be higher, but more accurate, indicators of the actual market for rental housing. Nevertheless, ownership of about half the property in the city made ecclesiastical corporations a convenient target for radicals seeking to alter the distribution of property. None of this need imply that liberals were solely or even predominantly concerned with their own private circumstances, but neither were the social and political realms entirely separated. Political convictions corresponded to social conditions.

Eight

Origins of Instability

in Mexico

Mexico's postindependence instability continues to be one of the most vexing enigmas faced by those who love Mexico. Central concerns of Mexican history, economics, politics, and culture are rooted in the trauma of those years. As politicians disputed the direction the new nation would take, Mexico lost half of its national territory. The Mexican economy faltered with consequences that are still felt today; most of the difference in productivity between the Mexican and U.S. economies dates from this period. Instability provided foreigners with a convenient justification for dismembering Mexico. It has been the basis for reactionary interpretations which would justify an authoritarian political tradition. Advocates for democracy have had to assert the rights of all people in the face of a history which seems to demonstrate the incapacity of some for self-government. The problems of the past may limit visions of a more egalitarian future.

There has been no consensus on the causes for the disorder that followed independence. Instability has resisted explanation, but the proliferation of competing hypotheses has left room for a simple, and pernicious, explanation. The identification of Mexico's history with the biography of Santa Anna cannot be justified, however convenient it makes the writing of textbooks. As Moisés González Navarro has reminded us, our task is not to explain Mexico in terms of Santa Anna, but to explain Santa Anna in terms of Mexico.[1] It is not the conspicuous knavery of a single general that requires attention, but the general conditions of economy, politics, and society. We need to refocus the history of early republican Mexico on the central tendency of relationships among economy, region, family, class, career, and politics. We need to know the essential rather than the anecdotal, the outlandish, or the extreme.

A more sophisticated explanation of Mexico's postindependence trauma has been hampered by the difficulties in sorting out the various effects of these multiple variables. We have myriad explanations which focus on distinct sorts of data relating to social class, region, family, politics, occupation, socialization, and global economic and fiscal conditions. A social science approach has the advantage of specifying hypotheses in ways that make them empirically testable. We are never able to confirm hypotheses, but we can evaluate the relative strength of groups of variables and reject those hypotheses that are not systematically consistent with the data. Conclusions, then, are more likely to require the rejection of false hypotheses than the confirmation of true ones. Those who would resuscitate one of these hypotheses will need to show alternate and superior data which systematically, not occasionally, resist rejection on this basis.

Explanations of instability on the basis of short-term economic conditions and fiscal resources specify relationships that can be evaluated in this way. Allowing for the variety of authors who have contributed to this interpretation, there are certain common assumptions and conclusions. The importance of political doctrines and affiliations have been questioned on two bases. Proponents of the caudillo thesis suggest that political discourse can be dismissed as superficial recitations designed to conceal crass ambitions; the caudillos' true motives were to use political posts to achieve prestige or to appropriate state funds to promote personal power. A more charitable view holds that economic and fiscal exigencies were so extreme that they demanded similar behavior from men with divergent political perspectives. In either case, governments were able to hold power longer when there were more funds in the treasury; when the fiscal fortunes of the state declined, power was likely to shift to another group. Instability resulted from economic fluctuations and fiscal constraints.

The evidence for such relationships is either ambiguous or contradictory. Low revenue collections and substantial borrowing did coincide with unusually unstable years, but these annual correlations cannot specify the direction of causation. Low revenues might as easily be the result of instability rather than its cause. Given this ambiguity, an economic origin for instability depends on the correlation between economic cycles, especially those in foreign trade, and political instability. This correlation has failed to materialize. Efficiency of collections seems to have little to do with instability. Governments that extracted relatively large taxes from foreign trade were as likely to be unstable as those which received only relatively small amounts. No systematic evidence shows that instability reflected the inadequacy of government revenues. The evidence that trade influenced political instability is not as strong as the data that tie the level of foreign trade to political decisions. Foreign commerce fluctuated with the level of trade taxes. As taxes were raised, trade declined. When taxes were reduced, foreign commerce increased.

It is also possible to set aside the notion that greater participation in government by social and economic elites would have permitted stabilization in Mexico. Most of the national executive elite was drawn from the highest 4 percent of the population resident in Mexico City, already the region with the highest concentration of wealthy and socially prominent families in Mexico. Mexico's presidents and cabinet ministers shared the space at the very top of the social hierarchy in the national capital. The argument that particular types—landowners, for example—were absent is only speculation. On the contrary, evidence suggests that greater participation by Mexico's social elite might have exacerbated instability rather than ameliorated it. Although those at the apex of society were likely to occupy national executive offices for more months during their lifetimes than those lower on the social ladder, the careers of the social elite were made up of individual terms that were shorter than average. Natives of the national capital were more likely to serve abbreviated rather than prolonged individual terms in office and to repeatedly pass in and out of government posts. But no one lasted very long in office during this period. The characteristics of individuals, including their political positions, experiences, education, training, and social background, seem to have had little systematic effect on the prevalence of political instability. The causes of instability may be more profitably sought in the broader social conditions of class and region.

A sociopolitical explanation suggests that political differences were rooted in economic and social variation. The origins of these elite politicians and their career patterns would reflect these differences in outlook and methods. Three major political factions with conflicting aims and overlapping methods sought solutions for Mexico's problems. Conservatives, moderates, and radicals differed in five areas: (1) state organization, (2) methods of social control, (3) state power and economic intervention, (4) Church-state relations, and (5) the value of the colonial experience.

Conservatives wanted a strong state, a monarchy with a centralized bureaucracy to enforce a hierarchical social structure and use deliberate state regulation and economic intervention to promote wealth and preserve privileges while resisting social mobility and change. Conservatives linked national identity to Catholicism and resisted Protestantism, Anglo-Saxonism, democracy, federalism, and other foreign germs of social degeneration. They wanted the Church to have a share in state power and to control birth, death, and marriage rituals and records. They believed that the colonial peace had been disrupted by foreign, liberal Bourbon monarchs who had increased colonial limitations on the wedding of private wealth and state power. They opposed Bourbon attempts to disestablish the Church and to weaken other privileges, to decentralize the royal bureaucracy, and to institute "free trade" policies which threatened their control of wealth and power. Their loyalty to Spain had weakened them politically and economically as the Bourbons extracted as much revenue as possible to defend Spain against the French Revolution and Napoleon.

Postindependence conservatives were not attempting to recreate the entire colonial state, but only those elements that had benefited them. Despite the reactionary rhetoric of some postindependence rural rebellions, conservatives did not consistently defend the rights of Indian villages, and they feared the participation of the rural classes in politics. Conservatives were too aware of the dangers of mobilizing the rural classes after their experience with the insurgency of 1810–1820. Most conservatives opposed even so much as the discussion of local autonomy until they seized on independence in 1821 as a way to avoid resurgent Spanish liberalism. Conservatives hoped to create a strong state by allying the Catholic Church with the national army, but they were frustrated by weaknesses in their plan and divisions within their coalition. Monarchists were unable to find a willing candidate for the throne after Iturbide's ethereal empire demonstrated that a dynasty could not be materialized out of pretense alone. Conservatives found that the army and the Church were not natural allies, despite the superficial similarities of concern to maintain their separate juridical privileges. Antonio López de Santa Anna was the embodiment of the militarist side of this contradiction. His efforts to find resources for his troops sometimes led him into alliances with radicals to weaken the Church. Santa Anna exceeded the conservatives in his extravagant attempts to increase state power, and surpassed even the radicals in his ruthless methods of extracting revenues from the Church and the wealthy.

Moderates were liberal, constitutional monarchists who felt uncomfortable with a republic, which they identified with mob rule and the French Reign of Terror. Moderates supported juridical equality, constitutions, and freedom of the press. They opposed monopoly and state intervention in the economy and tolerated foreign capital. They wanted a weak state which would not inhibit the free exercise of their economic power. Moderates agreed in principle to some limitations on the Catholic Church's power but thought that any reform ought to be slow and gradual and should not under any circumstances erode the right to property which, for them, was the basis of civilization. Moderates recognized their ties to the reforms of the Spanish Enlightenment, but some had supported independence to avoid the consequences of revolution in Europe.

For radicals, the republic was a requirement for social progress. They wanted a strong state to limit privilege and support concessions to the urban lower class by providing protection from foreign competition and expelling foreign merchants. Many radicals believed economic development ought to take place in an environment of controlled competition. A strong state was a requirement to destroy the social and political power of the Church and to reform rural society, which radicals regarded as the product of ignorance and racism inherited from the colonial regime. Radicals hoped to end the domination of the countryside by retrograde institutions left over from the colonial period. Some radicals sponsored plans to divide haciendas and provide land to the rural poor, but radicals did not regard the hacienda as the only obstacle to progress in rural

Mexico. They regarded the communal village and the special status of Indians as oppressive institutions; radicals repeatedly decreed the legal end of communal land tenure and the beginning of legal equality for all citizens. Some radicals attempted to mobilize the urban populace in support of their policies, but this constituency was not as powerful as those of the moderates and conservatives.

Patterns in the socialization and background of presidents and cabinet ministers from 1824 to 1867 support the general outlines of this thesis. Substantial numbers of the postindependence political elite simply waited out the struggles for independence, but among those who did take up arms, there were consistent patterns. Postindependence radicals were the political heirs of the insurgency of 1810–1820. Radicals were the most likely to have supported the armed insurgency led by Hidalgo and Morelos. Moderates could have been found on either side of these wars: some clinging to their hopes for enlightened monarchy, some believing that independence offered the only hope to avoid European cycles of revolution and reaction. Conservatives were more clearly pro-Spanish; those who took part in the wars of the independence era almost invariably served in the Spanish army or the royalist militias.

After independence, the general lines of this conflict continued in the rivalry between the national army and the civic and state militias. Radicals were most likely to begin their military careers as citizen-soldiers; they hoped to use the militias to weaken the control of the army over politics. Conservatives were inclined to see the militias as filled with the worst social elements and as threats to property and state power. Nearly all conservatives who began military careers after independence took commissions in the national army. Moderates, ever mindful of the expense of a strong state, complained of the cost of the national army and its deplorable tendency to threaten the government rather than protect it. They hoped to avoid these excesses by restricting participation in the less costly militias to the propertied classes. Moderates typically avoided military service themselves; very few began military careers after independence.

Most moderates served a term in the national legislature before becoming president or cabinet ministers. This legislative experience reflected and reinforced their view of compromise and cooperation as the necessary means to consensus solutions and evolutionary reform. Radicals and conservatives were more likely to use state power to enforce solutions, and only a minority of these men served in the legislature before taking office as presidents and cabinet ministers. Both radicals and conservatives were more likely to begin their political careers in executive posts, but with an important distinction: radicals were more likely than moderates or conservatives to begin as state governors; conservatives were more likely to become cabinet ministers or even president without prior experience as legislators or governors.

In Mexico spatial distribution approximates social hierarchy. Historians have speculated that conservatives were more likely to come from families resident in the central region and that liberalism predominated in a crescent that surrounded the central core. Evidence of this geographical extension of politics has been sparse and anecdotal, but the hypothesis has much to commend it. The traditionally conservative capital had served as the seat of power for the Aztec empire, the colony of New Spain, and the national government of the Republic of Mexico. It produced a preponderance of conservative politicians, a fair number of moderates, and even a few radicals. The central region as a whole, including the areas usually considered the liberal crescent, were apparently ethnically and socially more complex. These states produced a diverse group of politicians distributed across the political spectrum. In both the South and the far North, the relationship between social structure and political ideology was evidently more direct. In the North, abundant land and the danger of attacks by migratory Indians might have eased social tensions. Ecclesiastical institutions were weak and the military served a clear social purpose. This coherent social climate produced liberals but relatively few conservatives. In the South, conflicts between sedentary Indian villages and the creole landowners were internal to society. The divisive social conflicts of the South produced a preponderance of radicals but proportionately fewer moderates or conservatives.

The distribution of birthplaces of the political elite also varied with the political importance of the locations. The great majority of each faction were born in urban areas, but moderates were roughly twice and radicals nearly three times as likely as conservatives to be born into families living in the countryside. Among those born in urban environments, there were important differences in the types of cities where their families lived. Conservatives were more likely than liberals to be born into families geographically closer to the centers of power. More than 70 percent of the conservatives were born to families living in the national or state capitals. Fewer than half of the moderates and only about a third of the radicals were born in the administrative centers.

These correlations between social geography and politics are strengthened by evidence tying political differences to social stratification in Mexico City. The national political elite was drawn almost entirely from the most prosperous 20 percent of the population, but within this stratum, the factions tended to occupy different positions. Radicals occupied the lowest levels of the social elite. They lived comfortably compared to the vast majority of the urban population, but their smaller households and few servants indicate their inferior social position. Conservatives, in contrast, were the most opulent and pampered. They tended to have the largest households and the greater number of servants, marking them among the most prosperous fraction of the population. Moderates tended to occupy the social space between the conservatives and radicals. Moderates were neither as affluent as the conservatives nor as nearly ordinary as the radicals.

The rents these families paid for their residences in Mexico City did not correspond neatly with either the size of their households or the number of live-in servants they employed. Moderates and conservatives could afford larger families and employed more servants, but they paid lower average monthly rents than the radicals. Natives of Mexico City also enjoyed substantial advantages in the housing market. This evidence is consistent with the hypothesis that family connections and business associations in the capital may have been important in reducing the sums the social elite spent on housing. This would be especially true for the conservatives and moderates with closer connections to the national capital. The Church charged higher rents to those in equal circumstances than did private landlords. If further investigation finds that the market for housing in Mexico City was skewed by preferential treatment among kin groups and business partners, ecclesiastical rents actually may have been closer to a competitive market equilibrium than rents charged by private owners. Nevertheless, radicals from the provinces were more likely to see Church ownership of half the property in the city as the principal obstacle to a free market.[2]

The correspondence between social conditions and political convictions suggests that the roots of postindependence political conflicts lie in the contradiction between political liberalism and the traditional social structure developed in the colonial period. The conflicts among radicals, moderates, and conservatives may have been the outcome of a transition from monarchy to a republic. The colonial system promoted and controlled social discord in order to maintain royal power. Royal manipulation of conflicts between social classes and corporate groups insured that power ultimately was reserved to the king, but the requirement that these groups be carefully balanced in the interests of social and political stability greatly restricted the state's freedom of action. Government reliance on these same corporate groups to insure high levels of income necessary to defend Spain against her European enemies reduced the state's relative autonomy and required considerable sacrifice from the colonial economy. Once independence was achieved, the centuries of balancing the interests of social groups produced a prolonged period of conflict before one vision of the new Mexico could predominate. Centuries of social manipulation by the monarchy made an orderly transition to republican institutions impossible.

The late colonial state was itself profoundly destabilizing. Aborted reforms confused and weakened the government bureaucracy while attempting to widen divisions between the economic and political elites. The later Bourbons hoped to create a homogeneous, unified political elite of peninsular Spaniards to allow the state a wider range of autonomy, but the reforms weakened the state rather than strengthening it. Wealthy Creoles were increasingly excluded from high political posts, while the Bourbons eagerly sold them military commissions in the expanded militias, ominously restricting conventional political influence while winking at abuses of extralegal military power. Reforms of commerce and government promised power and influence to new groups, but provincial elites were frustrated by the debasement of the reforms. New merchant guilds were chartered and the intendant system was inaugurated, but the old system which centralized economic and political power in Mexico City continued to struggle for power. The crown would neither strike the fatal blow to the old system nor allow the new one to be born.

Riots and revolts demonstrated the power of the lower classes when political and religious elites made their quarrels public. Regional revolts following the expulsion of the Jesuits in 1767 were suppressed only through the use of military force without precedent in Mexico since the days of Cortés. But the crucial element in setting off the wars for independence was the political instability of Europe. The abdications of Charles IV and Ferdinand VII in favor of Joseph Bonaparte widened divisions among New Spain's elites and destroyed the recognized method of conflict resolution—the aged, creaking, ponderously slow process of endless appeals to the king. As elites publicly debated alternative governments in 1808, the range of possibilities was fairly narrow; certainly no one went so far as to suggest independence, much less a republic. Although the differences were small, even a slight shift in such a precariously balanced system could be expected to have far-reaching consequences. Even minor change threatened the fragile stability of late colonial New Spain, and the status quo could not be maintained. Subsequent waves of constitutionalism, reaction, and reform from Europe swept over the turbulent political scene in Mexico until 1821 when Iturbide found consensus for his Plan of Iguala; everyone agreed Mexico would be unable to solve its problems until Spanish tides of instability were prevented from continually altering the country's political topography.

The failure of either liberals or conservatives to provide stable government after independence may be due to the heritage of the monarchy's shifting power and the correspondingly weakened, fragmented, and partial social bases which supported each political faction. This lack of correspondence between state and society is inherent in the rule of a king, but it is antithetical to elected government that represents rather than rules. Conservatives could blame instability on imported ideologies that contradicted Mexico's historical reality. Radicals could hope to use state power to reshape Mexican society to fit republican institutions. Neither could be entirely satisfied.

As competition between elites increased in the 1840s, rebellions in the countryside increasingly took advantage of the weakness of the state to take up arms against the plans of radicals to erase village land tenure and of moderates and conservatives to allow the expansion of hacienda agriculture. Rural rebellions weakened the repressive apparatus of the state by drawing off troops, contributing indirectly to the revolution of 1844. War with the United States coincided with widespread rural rebellions in Yucatán and the Sierra Gorda of Querétaro as well as Apache wars in northern Mexico. With Mexican forces so dispersed and occupied, General Scott's buckskin-clad troops hoisted the stars and stripes over Mexico's national palace.

Mexican politicians were stunned by their loss; fewer compromises were possible after the war. Coalitions were more difficult to form as each group blamed the others for the defeat. Moderates were discredited by their accession to the Treaty of Guadalupe Hidalgo ceding half the national territory to the United States. Radicals blamed the Church for failing to provide enough money to prevent defeat and regarded the bishops and militia leaders as traitors for rebelling when President Gómez Farías attempted to extract funds from the Church to pay for the war. Radicals grew more determined to end the Church's wealth and power to insure Mexico's survival as a republic. Conservatives blamed Mexico's weakness on social degeneration caused by liberal innovations. Conservatives rejected the Constitution of 1857 and declared war on their domestic enemies rather than accept provisions requiring legal equality of all citizens and divestment of Church property. Mexican conservatives who had longed for a monarch actively sought a European prince and European alliances to strengthen the state and defend Mexico against the United States. Moderates found their position increasingly untenable as they were forced to choose between monarchy and democracy, between treason and heresy. The complex political interactions of the early republican era became increasingly polarized; instability was transformed into civil war.

The Wars of the Reform and the French Intervention changed Mexico in ways neither liberals nor conservatives had planned. Radicals won the war, but they found themselves in charge of a large professional military force, facing problems of demobilization, increased local autonomy, and a shattered economy. The fiscal exigencies of ten years of war had emptied the treasury of the funds they had planned to use to reshape Mexican society. Radical plans to encourage economic growth with the resources of a disestablished Church were no longer possible since the proceeds of forced sales had been consumed in ten years of war. Church property had to be sold quickly to provide funds to republican forces, allowing large amounts of rural and urban property to pass into the hands of wealthy speculators, increasing inequality rather than creating a middle class. The defeat of conservative and French armies and the execution of Emperor Maximilian ended the dreams of conservatives for a Mexican monarchy. Some families lost their fortunes, but Mexico's economic elites emerged relatively stronger after the wars. The rural majority was weakened. Extension of the laws to end communal village land tenure increased social differentiation within Indian villages, reducing social cohesion and leaving the villages increasingly subject to the economic power of local landowners. Radicals had taken control of the government, but conservatives retained and expanded their economic power. Mexico would be a republic, the Church was disestablished, but economic and social reforms were thwarted. If instability resulted from the incompatibility of liberal politics with Mexico's degree of economic inequality and social hierarchy, Porfirio Díaz resolved the contradiction by providing monocracy as a substitute for monarchy. Setting the state once more above society provided stability in the absence of radical social change. Capitalism flourished, administration stabilized, and order triumphed over liberty.

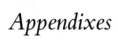

Appendixes

Name	Politics	Birthplace
Aguilar y Marocho, Ignacio	Conservative	Michoacán
Aguirre, José María	Moderate	Nuevo León
Alamán, Lucas	Conservative	Guanajuato
Alas, Ignacio	Conservative	Guanajuato
Alcaraz, Ramón Isaac	Radical	Michoacán
Alcorta, Lino José	Conservative	Veracruz
Alegría, Mariano	Conservative	Puebla
Almazán, Pascual	Conservative	DF
Almonte, Juan Nepomuceno	Conservative	Michoacán
Alvarez, Juan	Radical	Guerrero
Ampudia, Pedro	Radical	Cuba
Anaya, Juan Pablo	Radical	Jalisco
Anaya, Pedro María	Moderate	Hidalgo
Anievas, Ignacio	Conservative	DF
Arias, Juan de Dios	Radical	Puebla
Arista, Mariano	Moderate	S. Luis Potosí
Arrangoiz y Berzábel, Francisco	Conservative	Veracruz
Arriaga, Ponciano	Radical	S. Luis Potosí
Arrioja, Miguel Maria	Radical	Puebla
Arroyo, José Miguel	Conservative	Unknown
Arroyo, Luis	Conservative	DF
Balcárcel, Blas	Radical	DF
Baranda, Manuel	Conservative	Guanajuato
Barragán, Miguel	Conservative	S. Luis Potosí
Barrera, Ignacio de la	Santanista	DF
Basadre, José Ignacio	Radical	Veracruz
Baz, Juan José	Radical	Jalisco
Becerra y Jiménez, José María Luciano	Conservative	Veracruz
Bejarano, Mariano A.	Undetermined	Unknown
Berriozábal, Felipe	Radical	Zacatecas
Blanchot, Carlos	Undetermined	Unknown
Blanco, Miguel	Moderate	Coahuila
Blanco, Santiago	Conservative	Campeche
Blasco, José María	Undetermined	Querétaro
Bocanegra, José María	Moderate	Aguascalientes

Name	Politics	Birthplace
Bravo, Nicolás	Conservative	Guerrero
Bustamante, Anastasio	Moderate	Michoacán
Cacho, José	Conservative	Unknown
Camacho, Sebastián	Conservative	Veracruz
Campillo, Félix	Undetermined	Unknown
Campos, José Mariano	Undetermined	Unknown
Canalizo, Valentín	Santanista	Nuevo León
Cañedo, Juan de Dios	Moderate	Jalisco
Canseco, Manuel María	Conservative	DF
Carrera, Martín	Santanista	Puebla
Castañeda, Marcelino	Conservative	Unknown
Castaños, José María	Radical	Nayarít
Castillo, Crispiano del	Moderate	Jalisco
Castillo, Severo del	Conservative	DF
Castillo y Cos, Martín del	Conservative	Veracruz
Castillo y Lanzas, Joaquín M. del	Conservative	Veracruz
Castro, José	Undetermined	Spain
Ceballos, Juan Bautista	Moderate	Durango
Cendejas, Francisco de Paula	Moderate	Unknown
Cervantes, José María	Conservative	Michoacán
César, Francisco de Paula	Undetermined	Unknown
Comonfort, Ignacio	Moderate	Puebla
Corona, Antonio	Conservative	Unknown
Corral, Ignacio del	Undetermined	Unknown
Corral, Juan José del	Santanista	Unknown
Corro, José Justo	Conservative	Jalisco
Cortés y Esparza, José María	Moderate	Guanajuato
Couto, José Bernardo	Radical	Veracruz
Cuevas, Luis G.	Conservative	Mexico
Degollado, Santos	Radical	Guanajuato
Díaz, Isidro	Undetermined	Unknown
Díaz de la Vega, Rómulo	Conservative	DF
Díaz Noriega, José María	Undetermined	Mexico
Díez de Bonilla, Manuel	Conservative	DF
Doblado, Manuel	Radical	Guanajuato
Durán, José María	Undetermined	DF
Echeverría, Francisco Javier	Moderate	Veracruz
Echeverría, Pedro	Moderate	Michoacán
Elguero, Hilaro	Conservative	DF
Elorreaga, Francisco	Radical	Chihuahua
Emparan, José de	Radical	Veracruz

Name	Politics	Birthplace
Escudero y Echanove, Pedro	Moderate	Campeche
Esparza, Marcos	Radical	Zacatecas
Espinosa, José Ignacio	Conservative	Guanajuato
Espinosa de los Monteros, Juan José	Moderate	DF
Esteva, José Ignacio	Moderate	Veracruz
Esteva, José María	Conservative	Veracruz
Esteva y González, José Ignacio	Santanista	Veracruz
Facio, José Antonio	Conservative	Veracruz
Fagoaga, Francisco	Moderate	DF
Fernández de Jáuregui, Juan M.	Conservative	Unknown
Fernández del Castillo, Pedro	Conservative	Guanajuato
Flores, Bernardo	Moderate	S. Luis Potosí
Fonseca, José Urbano	Moderate	DF
Fuente, Juan Antonio de la	Radical	Coahuila
Garay, Antonio	Santanista	Veracruz
Garay y Garay, Pedro de	Radical	Veracruz
García, Antonio	Undetermined	Unknown
García, Carlos	Moderate	Puebla
García, José María	Conservative	DF
García Aguirre, Manuel	Conservative	DF
García Conde, José María	Moderate	DF
García Conde, Pedro	Moderate	Sonora
García Salinas, Francisco	Radical	Zacatecas
Garza, Juan José de la	Radical	Tamaulipas
Gochicoa, Francisco de Paula	Radical	DF
Godoy, Juan Ignacio	Undetermined	Unknown
Gómez Anaya, Cirilo	Conservative	Jalisco
Gómez de la Cortina, José	Conservative	DF
Gómez de Portugal y Solís, Juan C.	Conservative	Guanajuato
Gómez Farías, Valentín	Radical	Jalisco
Gómez Parada, Francisco	Undetermined	Unknown
Gómez Pedraza, Manuel	Moderate	Querétaro
Gómez Valdés, Pablo	Santanista	Veracruz
González de la Vega, José María	Undetermined	Unknown
González Echeverría, José	Radical	Puebla
González Ortega, Jesús	Radical	Zacatecas
González Pérez de Angulo, Bernardo	Moderate	Puebla
Gorostiza, Manuel Eduardo de	Radical	Veracruz
Guerrero, Vicente	Radical	Guerrero
Gutiérrez, Bonifacio	Moderate	Oaxaca
Gutiérrez, José Ignacio	Moderate	Chihuahua

Name	Politics	Birthplace
Gutiérrez Estrada, José María	Moderate	Campeche
Guzmán, Juan	Undetermined	Puebla
Guzmán, León	Radical	Mexico
Haro y Tamariz, Antonio	Conservative	Puebla
Herrera, José Joaquin de	Moderate	Veracruz
Herrera, José Manuel de	Radical	Tlaxcala
Hierro Maldonado, Juan	Conservative	Puebla
Hinojosa, Pedro	Radical	Tamaulipas
Horta, Antonio María	Undetermined	Puebla
Huici, José Luis	Conservative	DF
Ibarra, Domingo	Undetermined	Coahuila
Icaza, Antonio	Moderate	DF
Iglesias, José María	Moderate	DF
Iribarren, José María	Conservative	Sinaloa
Iturbe y Anciola, Francisco	Conservative	Michoacán
Iturbide, Joaquín	Undetermined	Unknown
Jáuregui, José Mariano	Undetermined	Veracruz
Jiménez, José María	Santanista	DF
Jorrín, Pedro	Undetermined	Guanajuato
Juárez, Benito	Radical	Oaxaca
Labastida y Dávalos, Antonio de	Conservative	Michoacán
Lacunza, José María	Conservative	DF
Ladrón de Guevara, José Joaquín	Moderate	DF
Lafragua, José María	Moderate	Puebla
Lares, Teodosio	Conservative	Aguascalientes
Larraínzar, Manuel	Conservative	Chiapas
Lebrija, Joaquín	Santanista	Veracruz
Lerdo de Tejada, Miguel	Radical	Veracruz
Lerdo de Tejada, Sebastián	Radical	Veracruz
Lombardini, Manuel María	Santanista	DF
Lombardo, Francisco María	Santanista	Hidalgo
López de Nava, Andres	Undetermined	Unknown
Llave, Ignacio de la	Moderate	Veracruz
Llave, Pablo de la	Moderate	Veracruz
Macedo, Mariano	Moderate	Jalisco
Mangino y Mendívil, Rafael	Conservative	Puebla
Maniau, Ildefonso	Undetermined	Veracruz
Marín, José Mariano	Undetermined	Puebla
Marín, Teófilo	Conservative	Puebla
Martínez, José Guadalupe	Undetermined	Unknown
Mata, José María	Radical	Veracruz

Name	Politics	Birthplace
Medina, Joaquin Antonio	Undetermined	Veracruz
Mejía, Ignacio	Radical	Oaxaca
Merino, Manuel María	Undetermined	Chihuahua
Michelena, José Mariano	Moderate	Michoacán
Mier y Terán, Joaquín	Conservative	DF
Mier y Terán, Manuel de	Moderate	DF
Miramón, Miguel	Conservative	DF
Miranda, Francisco Javier	Conservative	Puebla
Moctezuma, Francisco	Moderate	Guerrero
Montes, Ezequiel	Moderate	Querétaro
Montes de Oca, Demetrio	Moderate	Unknown
Mora y Villamil, Ignacio	Conservative	DF
Morán y del Villar, José	Moderate	Querétaro
Muñoz Ledo, Octaviano	Moderate	Guanajuato
Murphy, Thomas	Conservative	Veracruz
Múzquiz, Melchor	Radical	Coahuila
Negrete, Miguel	Undetermined	Puebla
Núñez, José Higinio	Radical	DF
Ocampo, Melchor	Radical	Michoacán
Ogazón, Pedro	Radical	Jalisco
Olazagarre, Manuel	Conservative	Jalisco
Ormaechea, Luis de	Undetermined	Unknown
Ormaechea y Ernaíz, Juan Bautista	Conservative	DF
Orozco y Berra, Manuel	Moderate	DF
Ortíz de la Torre, Manuel	Moderate	Sonora
Ortíz Monasterio, José María	Undetermined	DF
Otero, Mariano	Moderate	Jalisco
Pacheco, José Ramón	Santanista	Jalisco
Palacio y Magarola, Lucas de	Moderate	Hidalgo
Paredes y Arrillaga, Mariano	Conservative	DF
Parra, José María	Conservative	Unknown
Parres, Joaquín	Moderate	Guanajuato
Parres, Luis	Conservative	Guanajuato
Parrodi, Anastasio	Moderate	Cuba
Partearroyo, José G. de	Radical	Unknown
Pavón, José Ignacio	Conservative	Veracruz
Payno, Manuel	Moderate	DF
Peña y Peña, Manuel de la	Moderate	DF
Pereda, Juan Nepomuceno de.	Conservative	Spain
Pérez de Lebrija, Agustín	Undetermined	Veracruz
Pesado, José Joaquín	Conservative	Puebla

Name	Politics	Birthplace
Peza, Juan de Dios	Moderate	Unknown
Peza y Peza, Carlos	Conservative	Unknown
Piña y Cuevas, Manuel	Conservative	DF
Piquero, Ignacio	Undetermined	DF
Pizarro Suárez, Nicolás	Radical	DF
Portilla, Nicolás de la	Conservative	Veracruz
Prieto, Guillermo	Radical	DF
Quijano, Benito	Radical	Yucatán
Quintana Roo, Andrés	Moderate	Yucatán
Quintanar, Luis	Conservative	Jalisco
Ramírez, Ignacio	Radical	Guanajuato
Ramírez, José Fernando	Moderate	Chihuahua
Ramos Arizpe, Miguel	Moderate	Coahuila
Raygosa, Felipe	Undetermined	Unknown
Reigadas, Francisco Javier	Undetermined	Unknown
Rejón, Manuel Crescencio	Radical	Yucatán
Reyes, Isidro	Moderate	Querétaro
Rincón, Manuel	Conservative	Veracruz
Riva Palacio, Mariano	Moderate	DF
Robles Pezuela, Luis	Conservative	Unknown
Robles Pezuela, Manuel	Conservative	Guanajuato
Rodríguez, Juan de Dios	Moderate	Querétaro
Rodríguez Puebla, Juan	Radical	DF
Romero, José Antonio	Conservative	Unknown
Romero, Vicente	Radical	Unknown
Rondero, Juan	Moderate	Puebla
Rosa, Luis de la	Moderate	Zacatecas
Ruiz, Joaquín	Radical	Puebla
Ruiz, José María	Undetermined	Unknown
Ruiz, Manuel	Radical	Oaxaca
Sagaceta, Gabriel	Conservative	DF
Salas, José Mariano	Conservative	DF
Salazar Ilarregui, José	Conservative	Sonora
Salgado Albarrán, Tomás	Radical	Guanajuato
Sánchez Castro, Pedro	Undetermined	Unknown
Sánchez Navarro, Carlos	Conservative	Coahuila
Sandoval, Manuel María de	Moderate	Mexico
Santa Anna, Antonio López de	Santanista	Veracruz
Segura Arguëlles, Vicente	Undetermined	Veracruz
Sierra y Rosso, Ignacio	Santanista	Veracruz
Siliceo, Manuel	Moderate	Unknown

Name	Politics	Birthplace
Somera, Francisco	Conservative	Veracruz
Soto Ramos, Juan	Moderate	Veracruz
Suárez Iriarte, Francisco	Radical	DF
Suárez Navarro, Ignacio	Undetermined	Unknown
Suárez Navarro, Juan	Santanista	Unknown
Tavera, Ramón	Conservative	Guerrero
Terán Perido, Jesús	Radical	Aguascalientes
Tola, Luis	Conservative	DF
Tornel y Mendívil, José María	Santanista	Veracruz
Torres, Agustín	Undetermined	Unknown
Torres Larrainzar, Joaquín	Conservative	Unknown
Torres Torrija, Eduardo	Undetermined	Unknown
Torrescano, Gerónimo	Undetermined	Unknown
Tovar, Urbano	Conservative	Jalisco
Trigueros, Ignacio	Santanista	Veracruz
Ulíbarri, José D.	Undetermined	Unknown
Urquidi, José María	Moderate	DF
Vallejo, Antonio	Undetermined	Unknown
Velázquez de León, Joaquín	Conservative	DF
Vélez, Pedro	Moderate	Zacatecas
Vicaíno, Antonio	Undetermined	Unknown
Victoria, Guadalupe	Moderate	Durango
Vidaurri, Santiago	Moderate	Nuevo León
Viezca y Montes, Agustín	Radical	Coahuila
Villalba, Esteban	Undetermined	Unknown
Villamil, Lázaro	Undetermined	Veracruz
Yáñez, José María	Conservative	DF
Yáñez, Mariano	Moderate	DF
Zaldívar, José María	Conservative	DF
Zamacona y Murphy, Manuel María	Radical	Puebla
Zambrano, Juan	Radical	Unknown
Zaragoza, Ignacio	Radical	Texas
Zarco, Francisco	Radical	Durango
Zavala, Lorenzo de	Radical	Yucatán
Zubieta, Pedro	Undetermined	Jalisco
Zuloaga, Félix	Conservative	Sonora

Sources: *Diccionario Porrúa de historia, biografía y geografía de México*, 5th ed.; *Enciclopedia de México, 1967-1976*; Manuel García Purón, *México y sus gobernantes: biografías* (Mexico: Porrúa, 1964); Alberto Leduc, Luis Lara y Pardo, and Carlos Roumagnac, *Diccionario de geografía, historia y biografía mexicanas* (Paris: Librería de la Vda. de Ch. Bouret, 1910); Ireneo Paz, *Los hombres prominentes de México* (Mexico: "La Patria,"

1888); Carlos J. Sierra, *Historia de la administración hacendaria en México, 1821-1970* (Mexico: Secretaría de Hacienda y Crédito Público, 1970); Sergio Sierra Domínguez and Roberto Martínez Barreda, comps., *México y sus funcionarios* (Mexico: Cárdenas, 1959); Francisco Sosa, *Biografías de mexicanos distinguidos* (Mexico: Secretaría de Fomento, 1884); idem, *Efemérides históricas y biográficas,* 2 vols. (Mexico: G. A. Esteva, 1883).

Appendix B   Elite Politicians and Their Residences in Mexico City, 1848

Last names	First names	Origin	Marital Status
Alegría	Mariano	Provincial	Married
Anaya	Juan Pablo	Provincial	Married
Anievas	Ignacio	Mexico City	Widower
Arrioja	Miguel María	Provincial	Married
Arroyo	Luis	Mexico City	Single
Barrera	Ignacio de la	Mexico City	Married
Canseco	Manuel María	Mexico City	Single
Ceballos	Juan	Provincial	Married
Cervantes	José María	Provincial	Widower
Couto	José Bernardo	Provincial	Married
Cuevas	Luis Gonzaga	Provincial	Married
Díaz de la Vega	Romulo	Mexico City	Married
Díez de Bonilla	Manuel	Mexico City	Married
Durán	José María	Mexico City	Married
Elguero	José Hilario	Mexico City	Single
Espinosa de los Monteros	Juan José	Mexico City	Widower
Fernández del Castillo	Pedro	Provincial	Married
Fonseca	José Urbano	Mexico City	Married
Garay	Antonio	Provincial	Married
García	José	Mexico City	Single
García Aguirre	Manuel	Mexico City	Widower
García Conde	José	Mexico City	Married
Gochicoa	Francisco	Mexico City	Single
Gómez Pedraza	Manuel	Provincial	Married
Gorostiza	Manuel Eduardo	Provincial	Married
Herrera	José Joaquín de	Provincial	Widower
Hierro Maldonado	Juan	Provincial	Single
Iglesias	José María	Mexico City	Single
Jáuregui	José María	Mexico City	Married
Jorrín	Pedro	Provincial	Single
Lafragua	José María	Provincial	Single
Larraínzar	Manuel	Provincial	Married

Age	Politics	Rent/ Value	Owner	Cuartel	Manzana
43	Conservative	$27	Church	11	104
63	Radical	$15	Private	14	131
29	Conservative	$10	Private	13	122
41	Radical	$90	Church	29	219
28	Conservative	$7	Private	26	186
49	Santanista	$50	Church	1	6
49	Conservative	$39	Church	14	139
37	Moderate	$30	Church	5	43
32	Conservative	$60	Church	5	49
45	Radical	$22,500	Self	11	92
48	Conservative	$60	Private	14	130
44	Conservative	$27	Private	11	93
48	Conservative	$30,000	Self	1	4
48	Unknown	$33	Church	14	135
33	Conservative	$40	Church	1	5
80	Moderate	$30	Church	9	79
49	Conservative	$42	Private	14	129
56	Moderate	$40	Church	1	2
42	Unknown	$50	Church	5	41
33	Conservative	$10	Church	1	4
50	Conservative	$12,000	Self	1	13
47	Moderate	$41	Church	1	5
23	Radical	$25	Private	5	47
59	Moderate	$85	Church	1	4
49	Radical	$60	Church	14	129
56	Moderate	$46	Church	14	125
46	Conservative	$100	Church	1	4
25	Radical	$53	Church	7	61
53	Unknown	$8	Church	1	5
36	Unknown	(missing)	Self	3	30
35	Moderate	$46	Church	7	63
39	Conservative	$60	Private	3	77

Last names	First names	Origin	Marital Status
Lerdo de Tejada	Miguel	Provincial	Married
Lombardini	Manuel	Mexico City	Married
Marín	José Mariano	Mexico City	Married
Marín	Teófilo	Mexico City	Single
Ortíz Monasterio	José María	Mexico City	Married
Otero	Mariano	Provincial	Married
Palacio	Lucas	Provincial	Married
Pavón	José Ignacio	Provincial	Married
Pérez de Lebrija	Agustín	Mexico City	Married
Piña y Cuevas	Manuel	Mexico City	Married
Rodríguez Puebla	Juan	Mexico City	Married
Rondero	Juan	Mexico City	Married
Sagaceta	Gabriel	Mexico City	Married
Salas	Mariano	Mexico City	Married
Suárez Iriarte	Francisco	Mexico City	Married
Trigueros	Ignacio	Provincial	Married
Vélez	Pedro	Provincial	Widower
Villamil	José Lázaro	Provincial	Married
Zaldívar	José María	Mexico City	Single
Zubieta	Pedro	Provincial	Widower

Sources: Padrón Municipalidad de México (1848), Archivo del Antiguo Ayunta-

Age	Politics	Rent/ Value	Owner	Cuartel	Manzana
36	Radical	$90	Church	1	1
46	Santanista	$26	Church	2	16
36	Unknown	$80	Private	24	189
23	Conservative	$41	Church	17	150
48	Unknown	$70	Church	1	10
31	Moderate	$60	Private	7	62
34	Moderate	(missing)	Self	1	5
57	Conservative	$30	Private	13	122
60	Unknown	$61	Private	9	79
44	Conservative	$50	Church	14	125
50	Radical	$35	Church	14	131
46	Unknown	$14,000	Self	5	47
39	Conservative	$83	Church	14	124
51	Conservative	$60	Church	1	12
44	Radical	$60	Church	1	1
43	Santanista	$125	Church	14	131
61	Moderate	$50	Church	1	6
40	Unknown	$50	Private	5	50
28	Conservative	$16	Private	15	140
43	Unknown	$50	Church	1	1

miento, v. 3408–3409. For political categories, see chapter 3 and Appendix A.

Appendix C   Statistics

Descriptive Statistics

Mean: the arithmetic mean, commonly called the "average," is the sum of all observations divided by the number of observations.

Median: the midpoint of a distribution of values, the value that has the same number of observations above and below it.

Mode: the most common value observed.

Minimum: the lowest value observed.

Maximum: the highest value observed.

Standard Deviation: a measure of the dispersion of values around the mean. The standard deviation is the square root of the arithmetic mean of the squared deviations from the mean.

Measures of Association

Spearman's rho is a nonparametric measure of association, designed to determine whether two variables share a common rank order, or monotonic form. Spearman's rho is $+1.0$ whenever the rankings correspond exactly and -1.0 whenever they are exactly reversed. A value of zero indicates there is no relationship between the two variables. The formula for Spearman's rho, r_s, is

$$r_s = 1 - \frac{6\,\Sigma D^2}{N\,(N^2 - 1)}$$

where D is the difference in rank for each case, and N is the number of cases.

Kendall's tau is a nonparametric measure of association which measures the degree of association between the rank order of two variables by counting the number of times pairs of rankings appear in the same order, subtracting the number which are not in order, and adjusting so that the value of Kendall's tau is $+1.0$ whenever the rankings correspond exactly and -1.0 whenever they are exactly reversed. A value of zero indicates there is no relationship between the two variables. The formula for Kendall's tau, t_a, is

$$t_a = \frac{C - D}{\tfrac{1}{2}\,N(N - 1)}$$

where C is the number of pairs ordered the same way, and D is the number of pairs that are ordered oppositely.

Correlation coefficient, or Pearson's Product-moment correlation coefficient, symbolized by r, is a measure of how closely observed values resemble a regression line. An r of zero indicates that there is no linear relationship between the two variables. An r close to zero indicates little correspondence between the observed values and the regression line. As r approaches $+1.0$ or -1.0, the relationship between the regression line and the observations approaches perfection. A negative sign for r denotes an inverse relationship between the observed variables. For example, in table 2.4 instability decreases as tax revenues increase.

R-squared: the square of the correlation coefficient. Ranges from zero to 1.0 and measures the proportion of variation in the dependent variable "explained" by the independent variable or variables.

Cross-tabulations

Chi-square is a test of statistical significance of cross-tabulations. It is calculated by comparing the actual cell frequencies with those that would be expected if there were no relationship between the two variables. The expected cell frequencies are calculated by multiplying the respective row and column totals and dividing by the total number of cases. The formula for the expected cell frequency, f_e^i, is

$$f_e^i = \left(\frac{C_i r_i}{N} \right)$$

The formula for chi-square, x^2, is

$$x^2 = \sum_i \frac{(f_o^i - f_e^i)}{f_e^i}$$

The greater the differences between the expected and actual cell frequencies, the larger the resulting chi-square. If there is no relationship between the two variables in a cross-tabulation, the resulting chi-square will be the result of random variation. A small value for chi-square is assumed to result from random variation, but we can assume that large values are unlikely to result unless there is a relationship between the variables. The probability of chi-square ranges from zero to 1.0 and measures the likelihood that a large value of chi-square would result by chance when there is no relationship between the variables. This probability depends on the number of rows and columns in the table, or more precisely on the number of degrees of freedom. Degrees of freedom, DF, are determined by the formula

$DF = (r-1)(c-1)$

Tests of significance, like chi-square, are applicable only to making inferences from sample data to the general population. My assumption in this case is that the data used here, Mexican presidents and cabinet ministers, are a sample of Mexican politicians in this period.

Phi measures the strength of association for a 2×2 table. Phi adjusts chi-square for the number of cases, since the size of chi-square is directly proportional to the number of cases. Phi has a value of zero when there is no relationship between the variables and a value of $+1.0$ when the relationship between the variables is perfect. The formula for phi is

$$\Phi = \frac{ad - bc}{\sqrt{(a+c)(b+d)(a+b)(c+d)}}$$

where a, b, c, and d are the cell frequencies in a 2 by 2 table.

Cramer's V is a modified version of phi for larger tables which adjusts phi for the number of rows or columns in a table, whichever is smaller. It has a minimum value of zero, indicating no relationship, and can reach unity even when the number or rows is not equal to the number of columns. The formula for Cramer's V is

$$V = \left(\frac{\Phi^2}{\min(r-1), (c-1)}\right)^{1/2}$$

where $\min(r-1), (c-1)$ is either $r-1$ or $c-1$, whichever is smaller.

Analysis of Variance and Analysis of Covariance

Analysis of variance is a statistical technique that compares the effects of independent categorical divisions (called "factors") of a group on a continuous dependent variable measured at the interval level. Analysis of covariance also adjusts for continuous variables (called covariates).

Factors: nonmetric, that is, categorical variables.

Covariates: metric variables. Analysis of variance that includes covariates as well as factors is called analysis of covariance.

Grand Mean: the overall mean for all groups in an analysis of variance or covariance.

N: the number of cases or observations.

Unadjusted Deviations: variation from the grand mean for each category in a factor before the variation from other sources is considered.

Eta: the common correlation ratio for each factor. When squared it gives the percentage of variance explained by a factor. Eta^2 can range from zero (if there is no difference between the categories of a factor) to 1.0

(if there is some difference between the categories of a factor but no variability within each category of the factor).

Adjusted Deviations: variation from the grand mean for each category in a factor after the variation from other sources (factors or factors and covariates) is considered.

Beta: the partial correlation ratio associated with each factor when adjusted for the effects of other factors and covariates.

F: the ratio of variances between subgroups in a factor. If F is 1.0, the variations from the grand mean are equal. As the F ratio departs from 1.0, the differences are greater. The ratios of variances displayed here are two-tailed, that is, the smaller a number less than 1.0 and the larger a number greater than 1.0, the greater the difference between the means of the subgroups.

Significance of F: based on the assumption that the variances in the population are equal, this figure gives the probability that variation would occur randomly. As in all cases where I display the results of tests of significance in this work, it is on the assumption that the data used here are a sample of Mexican politicians in this period.

Sum of Squares: the total of squared deviations from the mean.

DF: the degrees of freedom associated with each factor.

Mean Square: the sum of squares divided by the degrees of freedom.

Sources: Hubert M. Blalock, *Social Statistics* (New York: McGraw-Hill, 1972); Charles M. Dollar and Richard J. Jensen, *Historian's Guide to Statistics: Quantitative Analysis and Historical Research* (New York: Holt, Rinehart & Winston, 1971); SPSS, Inc., *SPSSX: User's Guide* (Chicago: SPSS, Inc., 1986).

Notes

One Instability and History

1 Josefina Vázquez de Knauth, *Mexicanos y norteamericanos ante la guerra del 47* (Mexico: SepSetentas, 1970), p. 11.

2 John H. Coatsworth, "Obstacles to Economic Growth in Nineteenth-Century Mexico," *American Historical Review* 83 (1978): 80–100.

3 Edmundo O'Gorman, "Precedentes y Sentido de la Revolución de Ayutla," in *Seis estudios históricos de tema mexicano* (Xalapa: Universidad Veracruzana, 1960), p. 133. This interpretation was especially popular in the United States where it appeared to justify the annexation of Texas and the conquest of the northern half of Mexico.

4 Michael P. Costeloe, *Church Wealth in Mexico: A Study of the "Juzgado de Capellanías" in the Archbishopric of Mexico, 1800–1856* (Cambridge: Cambridge University Press, 1967), and his *La primera república federal en México, 1824–1835: (un estudio de los partidos políticos en el México independiente)* (Mexico: Fonda de Cultura Económica, 1975); Moisés González Navarro, *Anatomía del poder en México, 1848–1853* (Mexico: El Colegio de México, 1977); Charles A. Hale, *Mexican Liberalism in the Age of Mora, 1821–1853* (New Haven, Conn.: Yale University Press, 1968); Fernando Díaz Díaz, *Caudillos y Caciques: Antonio López de Santa Anna y Juan Alvarez* (Mexico: El Colegio de México, 1972); Barbara A. Tenenbaum, *The Politics of Penury* (Albuquerque: University of New Mexico Press, 1986); Stuart F. Voss, *On the Periphery of Nineteenth-Century Mexico: Sonora and Sinaloa, 1810–1877* (Tucson: University of Arizona Press, 1982); David J. Weber, *The Mexican Frontier, 1821–1846: The American Southwest Under Mexico* (Albuquerque: University of New Mexico Press, 1982).

For reviews of the major works on this period see, Robert A. Potash, "Historiography of Mexico since 1821," *Hispanic American Historical Review* 40 (1960): 383–424; Stephen R. Niblo and Laurens B. Perry, "Recent Additions to Nineteenth-Century Mexican Historiography," *Latin American Research Review* 13:3 (1978): 3–45; and Josefina Zoraida Vázquez, "Los Años Olvidados," *Mexican Studies/ Estudios Mexicanos* 5:2 (Summer 1989): 313–326.

5   In their recent synthesis of Mexican history, Meyer and Sherman summarized the period this way: "A series of governments more concerned with show than with development, officials pilfering the treasury with impunity, political factions rife with internal dissension, [and] an economy mired in its own inertia, all militated against progress. Time after time the country ignited in conflagration. Santa Anna himself must bear much of the responsibility. Often clever but never wise, he set an example of dishonesty, deception and complete failure to adhere to any set of principles. All of his loyalties were mercurial, and the tone he established for the age proved contagious." Michael C. Meyer and William L. Sherman, *The Course of Mexican History*, 3d ed., (New York: Oxford University Press, 1987), pp. 332–333. Others who share this evaluation of Santa Anna include Frank N. Samponaro, "Santa Anna and the Abortive Anti-Federalist Revolt of 1833 in Mexico," *The Americas* 40 (July 1983): 95–107; Leslie Byrd Simpson, "Santa Anna's Leg," in his *Many Mexicos* (Berkeley: University of California Press, 1941), pp. 202–226, reprinted in *Mexico, from Independence to Revolution, 1810–1910*, ed. W. Dirk Raat (Lincoln: University of Nebraska Press, 1982); Díaz Díaz, *Caudillos y caciques*; and Wilfred Hardy Callcott, *Santa Anna: The Story of an Enigma Who Once Was Mexico* (Norman: University of Oklahoma Press, 1936). Somewhat more evenhanded are Michael Costeloe (who described Santa Anna as a "chronic prevaricator"), "Santa Anna and the Gómez Farías Regime in Mexico, 1833–1834," *The Americas* 31 (July 1974): 44, and Jan Bazant (who concluded, "Sincere or not, he proved incompetent to govern the country."), *A Concise History of Mexico from Hidalgo to Cardenas, 1805–1940* (Cambridge: Cambridge University Press, 1977), p. 61. For a more favorable view of Santa Anna, see José C. Valadés, *Orígenes de la República mexicana, la aurora constitucional* (Mexico: Editores Mexicanos Unidos, 1972) and Valadés, *Santa Anna y la guerra de Téjas* (Mexico: Editores Unidos Mexicanos, 1965).

6   González Navarro, *Anatomía del poder*, pp. 1–2.

7   Narrative political analysis makes two principal assumptions: that political power is the ability to initiate or block potential action and that power is generalized in the system rather than varying significantly

from one issue to another. The selection of issues to be studied introduces the bias of the investigator, since as a practical matter only a few
issues can be studied in detail, while the power exercised in the resolution of those specific issues may not be generalized in the whole
political system. By choosing recognized public issues, this method
ignores power exercised in deciding the agenda and power exercised
in decisions made without public controversy. In fact, the noncontro-
versial nondecisions may tell us more than issues that attract public
attention. The power to prevent discussion of society's fundamental
relationships is conceivably a government's greatest power. Robert D.
Putnam, *The Comparative Study of Political Elites* (Englewood Cliffs,
N.J.: Prentice-Hall, 1976), p. 17.

8   For reviews of the classic models of revolution, see Rod Aya, "Theories of Revolution Reconsidered," *Theory and Society* 8 (1979): 39–99,
and Theda Skocpol, "Explaining Revolutions: In Quest of a Social
Structural Approach," in *Uses of Controversy in Sociology*, ed. Lewis A.
Coser and Otto N. Larsen (New York: Free Press, 1976). For a
thoughtful analysis of the revolutionary potential of early nineteenth-
century Mexico, see Hugh M. Hamill, Jr., "Was the Mexican Independence Movement a Revolution?" in *Dos revoluciones: México y los
Estados Unidos* (Mexico: Fomento Cultural Banamex, A.C., 1976),
pp. 43–61.

9   Costeloe, *La primera república federal*, and Stanley C. Green, *The Mexican Republic: The First Decade, 1823–1832* (Pittsburgh: University of
Pittsburgh Press, 1987).

10   Merle Kling, for example, notes 116 changes of executive in the first
126 years of Honduran history, four presidents in one month in
Ecuador, and eight finance ministers in eighteen months in Brazil.
Kling, "Towards a Theory of Power and Political Instability in Latin
America," *Western Political Quarterly* 9 (March 1956): 23. See also David
Sanders, *Patterns of Political Instability* (New York: St. Martin's Press,
1981), and Keith M. Dowding and Richard Kimber, "The Meaning
and Use of 'Political Stability,'" *European Journal of Political Research*
11 (September 1983): 229–243.

11   Richard N. Sinkin, *The Mexican Reform, 1855–1876: A Study in Liberal Nation-Building* (Austin: Institute of Latin American Studies, University of Texas, 1979), and his "The Mexican Constitutional Congress, 1856–1857: A Statistical Analysis," *Hispanic American Historical
Review* 53 (1973): 1–26; Peter H. Smith, *Labyrinths of Power: Political
Recruitment in Twentieth-Century Mexico* (Princeton, N.J.: Princeton
University Press, 1979).

12   "In complex systems, formal and informal relations of power and

coordination are likely to converge at the top. Organization theory suggests that even in small groups inefficiency increases sharply when formal and informal structures are discrepant." Putnam, *Comparative Study of Political Elites*, p. 18.

13 Studies which explicitly compared these techniques found that "power-as-reputation overlapped almost completely with power-as-position. Virtually everyone whose name appeared on the reputational lists was already in the positional sample. Moreover, the overlap between position and reputation was greatest in the governmental and (in Yugoslavia) party sectors, precisely the sectors of greatest centrality in terms of both reputation and political interaction. Where it matters most, it seems, the differences among the three techniques matter least." Ibid.

Two   Accounting for Caudillos

1 Robert A. Potash, *Mexican Government and Industrial Development in the Early Republic: The Banco de Avío* (Amherst: University of Massachusetts Press, 1983), p. 171. These problems have been addressed in Tenenbaum, *The Politics of Penury*.

2 Coatsworth, "Obstacles to Economic Growth," p. 95.

3 Jacques Lambert, *Latin America: Social Structure and Political Institutions* (Berkeley: University of California Press, 1967), p. 156. See also Kling, "Towards a Theory of Power and Political Instability in Latin America," pp. 21–35; Eric R. Wolf and Edward C. Hansen, "*Caudillo* Politics: A Structural Analysis," *Comparative Studies in Society and History* 9 (January 1967): 168–179; William H. Beezley, "*Caudillismo*: An Interpretive Note," *Journal of Interamerican Studies and World Affairs* 11 (July 1969): 345–352. While these authors would limit caudillismo to particular historical periods, Glen Caudill Dealy, *The Public Man: An Interpretation of Latin American and Other Catholic Countries* (Amherst: University of Massachusetts Press, 1977), in contrast, attributes the caudillo style to distinctly Catholic culture and tradition that has endured for centuries with a far broader geographic range.

4 Wolf and Hansen, "*Caudillo* Politics," pp. 173–176.

5 Ibid., p. 176. Bazant, *Concise History*, pp. 31, 41, 42; Henry B. Parkes, *A History of Mexico* (Boston: Houghton Mifflin, 1938), p. 179; and Francisco López Cámara, *La estructura económica y social de México en la época de la Reforma*, 4th ed. (Mexico: Siglo Ventiuno Editores, 1976), pp. 168–173, among others note the direct relationship between amounts in the treasury and political instability.

6 Torcuato S. Di Tella, "The Dangerous Classes in Early Nineteenth Century Mexico," *Journal of Latin American Studies* 5 (May 1973): 105.

7   Justo Sierra, *The Political Evolution of the Mexican People*, trans. Charles Ramsdell (Austin: University of Texas Press, 1969), p. 191.

8   To cite only two recent examples: David Weber counted thirty-six changes between 1833 and 1855 while Florencia Mallon found only fourteen alternations in three decades. David J. Weber, *Myth and the History of the Hispanic Southwest* (Albuquerque: University of New Mexico Press, 1988), p. 109; Florencia Mallon, "Peasants and State Formation in Nineteenth-Century Morelos," *Political Power and Social Theory* 7 (1988): 1–54.

9   Bwy found that elite instability was positively correlated with social turmoil during the same period and was positively correlated with the outbreak of civil war at a later time. Douglas P. Bwy, "Dimensions of Social Conflict in Latin America," in *When Men Revolt, and Why*, ed. James Chowning Davies (New York: Free Press, 1971), pp. 284–285.

10 Mexico passed through a period of political instability and elite fragmentation until 1858, after which the polarization of elites was demonstrated by the continued existence of parallel governments complete with competing heads of state and cabinet officers from January 1858 to December 1860 and again from June 1863 to May 1867.

11 Obviously the total number of changes in the national executive offices will also depend on the end points chosen. Some of the data used in the tables which follow were not available for the years after 1844. Gaps in financial reports during the war years and in series of foreign trade data in the early 1850s were particularly troublesome. To make the tables and tests comparable and to avoid confusing effects of the war with the United States with variations of different series, it is necessary that the same years be used consistently. Each of the following statistical tests uses all years prior to 1844 for which data are available.

12 The total number of annual changes in table 2.1 and the following tables is the simple arithmetic sum of all alterations in the presidency and the cabinet for a given calendar or fiscal year. Thus, the substitution of an interim president for the constitutional president would count as 1, as would the resignation of any cabinet minister. If the president and his entire cabinet resigned and were replaced only once in any year, the sum would be 6. Only the year 1831 registered no changes in the presidency or the cabinet.

13 For explanations of the statistics, see Appendix C.

14 See Jan Bazant, *Historia de la deuda exterior de México, 1823–1946* (Mexico: El Colegio de México 1968); Tenenbaum, *The Politics of Penury*; Reinhard Liehr, "La deuda exterior de Mexico y los 'merchant bankers' británicos, 1821–1860," *Ibero-Amerikanisches Archiv* N.F.

9:3/4 (1983): 415–439; and *Formación y desarrollo de la burgesía en México. Siglo xix* (Mexico: Siglo Veintiuno, 1981).

15 It makes little difference whether foreign and domestic borrowing are considered separately or together as in table 2.3. With only domestic borrowing compared to executive instability: Spearman's rho = 0.398, Kendall's tau = 0.242, correlation coefficient = 0.381, r^2 = 0.145. If the percentage of total government income that came from loan proceeds is compared with executive instability: Spearman's rho = 0.361, Kendall's tau = 0.222, correlation coefficient = 0.423, r^2 = 0.179. Nor does using the log of total borrowing make much difference: correlation coefficient = 0.411, r^2 = 0.169.

16 For a clear discussion of the relationship among value, utility, and price, see Joan Robinson, *Economic Philosophy* (Harmondsworth, Eng.: Penguin, 1978), chaps. 2–3.

17 See, for example, Gabriel Ardant, "Financial Policy and Economic Infrastructure of Modern States and Nations," and Rudolph Braun, "Taxation, Sociopolitical Structure and State-Building in Great Britain and Brandenberg-Prussia," in *The Formation of National States in Western Europe*, ed. Charles Tilly (Princeton, N.J.: Princeton University Press, 1975), pp. 164–327; and Witold Kula, *Economic Theory of the Feudal System* (New York: NLB, 1976).

18 Wolf and Hansen, "*Caudillo* Politics," p. 171.

19 Marcello Carmagnani, "Finanzas y estado en Mexico, 1820–1880"; *Ibero-Amerikanisches Archiv* N.F. 9:3/4 (1983): 290–291.

20 Hindricks, "Determinants of Government Revenue Share in Less-Developed Countries," *Economic Journal* 75 (September 1965): 546–556. See also Vito Tanzi and Clayton McCuiston, "Determinants of Government Revenue Share in Less-Developed Countries: A Comment," *Economic Journal* 77 (June 1967): 403–405; Alan R. Roe, "Determinants of Government Revenue Share in Poorer African Countries: A Comment," *Economic Journal* 78 (June 1968): 478–481. For alternative measures, see Jorgen R. Løtz and Elliot R. Morss, "Measuring 'Tax-Effort' in Developing Countries," *Staff Papers* (International Monetary Fund) 14 (1967): 478–497.

21 "Taxes on the 'External' Sector: An Index to Political Behavior in Latin America?" *Midwest Journal of Political Science* 3 (May 1959): 127–150.

22 Ibid., p. 149.

23 Ibid.

24 Tenenbaum, *The Politics of Penury*, p. 174.

25 Ibid., pp. 25–29. See also Michael P. Costeloe, "The Triangular Revolt in Mexico and the Fall of Anastasio Bustamante, August–October

1841," *Journal of Latin American Studies* 20 (1980): 345, 347.

26 *Memoria de la Hacienda nacional de la República mexicana* (Mexico, 1841), p. 6, cited by Carmagnani, "Finanzas y estado," p. 289.

27 Warren Dean, "Latin American *Golpes* and Economic Fluctuations, 1823–1966," *Social Science Quarterly* 51 (June 1970): 70–80. For a study with a broader definition of instability and a more precise focus on economic cycles in Argentina, see Gilbert W. Merkx, "Recessions and Rebellions in Argentina, 1870–1970," *Hispanic American Historical Review* 53 (May 1973): 285–295.

28 Coatsworth, "Obstacles to Economic Growth," p. 82.

29 There are no good official estimates of Mexico's total imports until the late nineteenth century. The most recent volume on Mexico's foreign trade in this period includes trade figures for only a few years. Inés Herrera Canales, *El comercio exterior de México, 1821–1875* (Mexico: El Colegio de México, 1977). The estimates displayed in table 2.6 and subsequently may be reasonable approximations and are based on the following assumptions. First, that the bulk of Mexico's imports came from the United States, Great Britain, and France. Second, since Mexico reportedly suffered from considerable contraband imports, that these imports should be measured as they leave the ports of Mexico's trading partners rather than as they are brought, legally or illegally, into Mexican territory. I have used estimates of exports to Mexico collected by the governments of the United States, France, and Great Britain. Government officials in these countries presumably had no interest in whether goods exported from their jurisdictions were imported into Mexico in conformity with Mexican trade regulations or not. Miguel Lerdo de Tejada apparently had access to these figures and published them in his *Comercio esterior de México* (Mexico: Impreso por R. Rafael, 1853). Robert A. Potash discovered an error in Lerdo's use of the British exports to Mexico. See, "El 'Comercio Esterior de México' de Miguel Lerdo de Tejada: Un Error Estadístico," *Trimestre Económico* 20 (1953): 474–479. I have used British export figures from G. R. Porter, *The Progress of the Nation, in Various Social and Economic Relations, from the Beginning of the Nineteenth Century*, 3d ed. (London: John Murray, 1851), pp. 362–367. Lerdo's figures for French exports to Mexico are from the French *Tableau Decennal*. See Jürgen Schneider, *Frankreich und die Unabhängigkeit Spanisch-Amerikas: zum französischen Handel mit den entstehenden Nationalstaaten (1810–1850)*, 2 vols. (Stuttgart: Klett-Cotta, 1981), 2:369–373. Lerdo's figures for U.S. exports to Mexico conform to the U.S. estimates published in U.S. Department of Commerce, *Historical Statistics of the United States from Colonial Times to*

1970, 2 vols. (Washington, D.C.: U.S. Government Printing Office, 1975): 2:903–907. Among other defects, the U.S. figures do not include overland trade with Mexico. On the limitations and qualifications of these figures and much more, see Richard J. Salvucci, "Aspects of United States–Mexico Trade, 1825–80: A Preliminary Survey" (unpublished paper presented at the annual meeting of the American Historical Association, Chicago, 1986).

30 Nor is there a systematic relationship between rising or falling trade and instability. Eight years conform to a hypothesis that rising trade would result in low instability and that high instability would coincide with falling trade (two years when rising trade coincided with low instability: 1830 and 1843; and six when falling trade coincided with high instability: 1829, 1832, 1834, 1837, 1838, 1841). More years contradict this hypothesis than support it: four when trade rose amid high instability (1833, 1835, 1839, 1844) and five when trade fell despite low instability (1828, 1831, 1836, 1840, 1842).

31 Consult note 29 above.

32 For a description of political conflicts over tariffs in this period, see Potash, *Mexican Government and Industrial Development*, pp. 12–38. See also Costeloe, "Triangular Revolt," pp. 340–341.

Three Political Conflict in Early Republican Mexico

1 D. A. Brading, "Creole Nationalism and Mexican Liberalism," *Journal of Interamerican Studies and World Affairs* 15 (May 1973): 161, or *The Origins of Mexican Nationalism* (Cambridge: Centre of Latin American Studies, University of Cambridge, 1985), p. 81.

2 Vázquez, "Los Años Olvidados," p. 314.

3 *El Universal*, 1 November 1853, cited by Charles A. Hale, "The War with the United States and the Crisis in Mexican Thought," *The Americas* 14 (October 1957): 166. Hale, *Mexican Liberalism*, pp. 163–168.

4 Mexican liberals were more influenced by French rationalists than by the English liberal tradition. José Miranda, "El liberalismo mexicano y el liberalismo europeo," *Historia mexicana* 8 (abril–junio 1959): 512–523. Jesús Reyes Heroles, *El liberalismo mexicano*, 3 vols. (Mexico: UNAM, 1957–1961), draws crucial distinctions between various currents in Mexican liberalism from the 1820s to the 1870s.

5 Hale, *Mexican Liberalism*, p. 123. Reyes Heroles, *El liberalismo mexicano*, 2:194, 275, 279.

6 Brian Hamnett, "Mexico's Royalist Coalition: The Response to Revolution," *Journal of Latin American Studies* 12 (May 1980): 79–84.

7   Michael P. Costeloe, "The Mexican Church in the Rebellion of the Polkos," *Hispanic American Historical Review* 46 (May 1966): 170–178; Mariano Cuevas, *Historia de la nación mexicana* (Mexico: Talleres Tipográficos Modelo, S.A., 1940), pp. 567–571; Hale, "Crisis in Mexican Thought," p. 160; González Navarro, *Anatomía*, pp. 9–10, 87–118, 427–431; Guillermo Prieto, *Memorias de mis tiempos*, 2 vols. (Mexico: Vda. de Ch. Bouret, 1906), 2:199–205; Frank N. Samponaro, "La Alianza de Santa Anna y los federalistas—1832–1834—su formación y desintegración," *Historia mexicana* 30 (enero–marzo 1981): 372–374; Niceto de Zamacois, *Historia de Méjico, desde sus tiempos mas remotos hasta nuestros dias*, 22 vols. (Barcelona and Mexico: J. F. Parres, 1880), 12:5–46.

8   Charles A. Hale, "The Reconstruction of Nineteenth Century Politics in Spanish America: A Case for the History of Ideas," *Latin American Research Review* 8 (Summer 1973): 60. See also Frederick Stirton Weaver, "Political Disintegration and Reconstruction in 19th Century Spanish America: The Class Basis of Political Change," *Politics and Society* 5:2 (1975): 161–183.

9   On the dialectical relationship between liberalism and conservatism, see the eloquent discussion by Edmundo O'Gorman, *México: El trauma de su historia* (Mexico: Universidad Nacional Autónoma de México, 1977), especially pp. 23–38. On the division between radicals and moderates over means and ends, see Brading, "Origins," pp. 70–76, or "Nationalism and Liberalism," pp. 145–153. On the increasingly dictatorial nature of Juárez's government, see Laurens B. Perry, *Juárez and Díaz: Machine Politics in Mexico* (DeKalb: Northern Illinois University Press, 1978).

10 Hale, *Mexican Liberalism*, pp. 163–168; François Chevalier, "Conservateurs et libéraux au Mexique: Essai du sociologie et géographie politiques de l'indépendance a l'intervention française," *Cahiers d'Histoire Mondiale* 8 (1964): 457–458; T. G. Powell, *El liberalismo y el campesinado en el centro de México (1850 a 1876)* (Mexico: SepSetentas, 1974), p. 16.

11 Lucas Alamán, *Historia de México desde los primeros movimientos que prepararon su independencia en el año de 1808 hasta la época presente*, 5 vols. (Mexico: J. Mariano Lara, 1850; facsimile ed., Mexico: Fondo de Cultura Económica, 1985), 5:855.

12 Quoted by Moisés González Navarro, *El pensamiento político de Lucas Alamán* (Mexico: El Colegio de Mexico, 1952), pp. 130, 147.

13 Barbara A. Tenenbaum, "Merchants, Money and Mischief: The British in Mexico, 1821–1862," *The Americas* 35 (January 1979: 317–340.

14 Hale, *Mexican Liberalism*, pp. 16, 248–249; Potash, *Mexican Govern-*

ment and Industrial Development; José C. Valadés, *Alamán, estadista e historiador* (Mexico: José Porrúa e Hijos, 1938), pp. 374–399.

15   González Navarro, *Anatomía*, p. 169; Dennis E. Berge, "A Mexican Dilemma: The Mexico City Ayuntamiento and the Question of Loyalty," *Hispanic American Historical Review* 50 (May 1970): 241–242, 247–248; Miguel Lerdo de Tejada, *El comercio esterior de México, desde la conquista hasta hoy* (Mexico: R. Rafael, 1853), pp. 31–34; Donathon C. Olliff, "Mexico's Mid-Nineteenth-Century Drive for Material Development," *Annals of the Southeastern Council of Latin American Studies* 8 (March 1977): 19–29.

16   Hale, *Mexican Liberalism*, p. 257; Potash, *Mexican Government and Industrial Development*, pp. 29–32; Harold D. Sims, La expulsión de los españoles de México *(1821–1828)* (Mexico: Fondo de Cultura Económica, 1974), p. 83; Romeo Flores Caballero, *Counterrevolution: The Role of the Spaniards in the Independence of Mexico, 1804–1828*, trans. Jaime E. Rodríguez O. (Lincoln: University of Nebraska Press, 1974), pp. 81–132; Rodríguez O. "Del libre cambio al proteccionismo," *Historia Mexicana* 19 (abril–junio 1976): 492–512; Frederick Shaw, "The Artisan in Mexico City (1824–1853)," in Frost, Vázquez, and Meyer, eds. *El trabajo y los trabajadores*, pp. 399–418.

17   Costeloe, *Church Wealth in Mexico*, p. 2.

18   Anne Staples, *La iglesia en la primera república federal mexicana* (Mexico: SepSetentas, 1976), pp. 35–73; Michael P. Costeloe, *Church and State in Independent Mexico—A Study of the Patronage Debate, 1821–1857* (London: Royal Historical Society, 1978).

19   W. Eugene Shiels, "Church and State in the First Decade of Mexican Independence," *Catholic Historical Review* 28 (July 1942): 206–211; Staples, *La iglesia*, pp. 18–31.

20   Mariano Otero, *Ensayo sobre el verdadero estado de la cuestión social y política que se agita en la República mexicana* (Mexico: Ignacio Cumplido, 1842), p. 43; Staples, *La iglesia*, pp. 97–126; Michael P. Costeloe, "The Administration, Collection, and Distribution of Tithes in the Archbishopric of Mexico, 1810–1860," *The Americas* 23 (July 1966): 3–27; Charles W. Macune, Jr., *El Estado de Mexico y la Federación mexicana, 1823–1835* (Mexico: Fondo de Cultura Económica, 1978), pp. 136–145.

21   Michael P. Costeloe, "Guadalupe Victoria and a Personal Loan from the Church in Independent Mexico," *The Americas* 25 (January 1969): 223–246; Costeloe, *Church Wealth in Mexico*, pp. 7, 9, 23.

22   Christon L. Archer, *The Army in Bourbon Mexico, 1760–1810* (Albuquerque: University of New Mexico Press, 1977); Lyle N. McAlister, *The "Fuero Militar" in New Spain, 1764–1800* (Gainesville:

University of Florida Press, 1957); María del Carmen Velázquez, *El estado de guerra en Nueva España, 1760–1808* (Mexico: El Colegio de México, 1950).

23   Pedro Santoni, "A Fear of the People: The Civic Militia of Mexico in 1845," *Hispanic American Historical Review* 68:2 (May 1988): 268–288; Ray F. Broussard, "The Mexican Liberals and the Curbing of the Military's Powers: Success or Failure?" *Annals of the Southeastern Conference on Latin American Studies* 10 (March 1979): 5–14; González Navarro, *Anatomía*, pp. 115–116, 120, 438; Samponaro, "La Alianza," p. 375.

24   Richard Packenham to Lord Palmerston, 11 June 1833, Great Britain, Public Record Office, Archives of the Foreign Office, Mexico (F.O. 50), vol. 79, ff. 241–246, cited by Di Tella, "The Dangerous Classes," p. 80.

25   Francisco de Paula de Arrangoiz y Berzábel, *México desde 1808 hasta 1867*, 4 vols. (Madrid: Imprenta a cargo de Estrada, 1871–1872), pp. 217–218.

26   Frederick Shaw, "Poverty and Politics in Mexico City, 1824–1854" (Ph. D. dissertation, University of Florida, 1975), pp. 330–331.

27   Prieto, *Memorias*, 2:199.

28   Cuevas, *Historia de la nación*, p. 593; Samponaro, "La alianza," pp. 380–390; Zamacois, *Historia de Méjico*, 12:251–252, 258–268, 271, 286–291, 297–301, 328, 334–335, 345–357.

29   Samponaro, "La Alianza," pp. 358–390.

30   Costeloe, "Rebellion of the Polkos," pp. 170–178.

31   Zamacois, *Historia de Méjico*, 12: 254–261, 297, 300.

32   Lucas Alamán to Antonio López de Santa Anna, 23 March 1853, cited by Hale, "Crisis in Mexican Thought," p. 168. Alamán apparently was fond of this formulation; the same phrase appears in his *Historia de México*, 5:929.

33   Nettie Lee Benson, "The Contested Mexican Election of 1812," *Hispanic American Historical Review* 26 (August 1946): 339–350.

34   José María Luis Mora, *Méjico y sus revoluciones*, 4 vols. (Paris: Librería de Rosa, 1836), 1:285–286. Hale, *Mexican Liberalism*, p. 95–98.

35   Alamán, *Historia de México*, 5:857.

36   Shaw, "Poverty and Politics," pp. 320–321. In 1843 suffrage was further restricted to those with annual incomes above 200 pesos, double the requirement of 1836. Herbert Ingram Priestley, *The Mexican Nation, A History* (New York: Macmillan, 1924), pp. 272–274, 295–296.

37   Valentín Gómez Farías to José María Luis Mora, 23 April 1844, in *Documentos inéditos ó muy raros para la historia de México*, ed. Genaro García (Mexico: Librería de la Vda. de Ch. Bouret, 1906), vol. 6: *Papeles inéditos y obras selectas del Doctor Mora*, p. 45.

38　Gómez Farías to Mora, 29 August 1846, in García, *Documentos*, 6:59.
39　Shaw, "Poverty and Politics," p. 342, and chapter 6. Di Tella, "Dangerous Classes," pp. 79–105.
40　Lorenzo de Zavala, *Juicio imparcial sobre los acontecimientos de México en 1828–1829* (New York: C.S. Van Winkle, 1830), pp. 29–41. For a conservative view of the Acordada Revolt and the Parián riot, see José María Tornel y Mendívil, *Breve reseña mexicana desde el año 1821 hasta nuestros dias* (Mexico: Imprenta de Cumplido, 1852), p. 348–392. Accounts differ on whether the radicals encouraged this attack on their enemies using the promise of booty to gain the allegiance of the mobs who supported them. See Silvia M. Arrom, "Popular Politics in Mexico City: The Parián Riot, 1828," *Hispanic American Historical Review* 68:2 (May 1988): 245–268; Harold D. Sims, *Descolonización en México: El conflicto entre mexicanos y españoles (1821–1831)* (Mexico: Fondo de Cultura Económica, 1982), pp. 74–89. On Gómez Farías and the Mexico City crowd from 1833 to 1845, see Zamacois, *Historia de Méjico*, 12:32–33, 46, 124–210, 356–364; Carlos María de Bustamante, *El gabinete mexicano durante el segundo periodo de la administración del exmo. señor presidente D. Anastasio Bustamante, hasta la entrega del mando al exmo. señor presidente interino D. Antonio López de Santa Anna*, 2 vols. (Mexico: J. M. Lara, 1842), 2:45–50; Carlos María de Bustamante, *Apuntes para la historia del gobierno de general D. Antonio López de Santa Anna, 1841–1844* (Mexico: J. M. Lara, 1845), p. 33; Michael P. Costeloe, "A Pronunciamiento in Nineteenth Century Mexico: '15 de julio de 1840,'" *Mexican Studies/Estudios Mexicanos* 4:2 (Summer 1988): 245–264; Cuevas, *Historia de la nación*, pp. 584–585. The Gómez Farías quote is from Valentín Gómez Farías to José María Luis Mora, 23 April 1844, in García, *Documentos inéditos*, 6:47. The Prieto quote is found in his *Memorias*, 2:160.
41　Shaw, "Poverty and Politics," pp. 323–324.
42　Costeloe, "Rebellion of the Polkos," pp. 170–178.
43　Berge, "Mexican Dilemma," p. 239.
44　González Navarro, *Anatomía*, pp. 224–225; Shaw, "Poverty and Politics," pp. 325, 346–348; Zamacois, *Historia de Méjico*, 13:339.
45　José Miranda, "La propiedad comunal de la tierra y la cohesión social de los pueblos indígenas mexicanos," *Cuadernos Americanos* 149 (noviembre–diciembre 1966): 169–177; Silvio Zavala and José Miranda, "Instituciones indígenas en la colonia," *Métodos y resultados de la política indigenista en México. Memorias del Instituto Nacional Indigenista* 6 (1954): 73–85; John H. Coatsworth, "The Limits of Colonial Absolutism: The State in Eighteenth Century Mexico," in *Essays in the Political, Economic and Social History of Colonial Latin America*, ed.

Karen Spaulding, (Newark: University of Delaware Press, 1982), pp. 28–29.

46 Donald J. Frazer, "La política de desamortización en las comunidades indígenas—1856–1872," *Historia mexicana* 21 (abril–junio 1972): 618–619; Jean Meyer, *Problemas campesinos y revueltas agrarias (1821–1910)* (Mexico: SepSetentas, 1971), p. 116.

47 Brian R. Hamnett, "Obstáculos a la política agraria del despotismo ilustrado," *Historia mexicana* 20 (julio–septiembre 1976): 55–75.

48 Frazer, "Desamortización," pp. 618–619; Robert J. Knowlton, "La individualización de la propiedad corporativa civil en el siglo xix—notas sobre Jalisco," *Historia Mexicana* 28 (julio–septiembre 1978): 26–27.

49 Ibid. Hamnett, "Consolidación," pp. 97–98; Miranda, "Propiedad comunal," pp. 87–88.

50 Quoted by Frazer, "Desamortización," p. 620.

51 Luis González y González, "El agrarismo liberal," *Historia mexicana* 7 (abril–junio 1958): 469–496.

52 Frazer, "Desamortización," pp. 622–623. Every state except Oaxaca also declared all towns to be uniformly equal.

53 Ibid., p. 623. Knowlton, "Individualización," p. 27.

54 González Navarro, *Anatomía*, p. 142; Frazer, "Desamortización," p. 622; Knowlton, "Individualización," pp. 27–28.

55 González Navarro, *Anatomía*, pp. 143–145. The Jalisco decree of 12 February 1825 was similar; see Knowlton, "Individualización," p. 29.

56 González Navarro, *Anatomía*, pp. 142–143; Miranda, "Propiedad comunal," p. 178. Meyer notes that the laws in Jalisco requiring division of communal lands were repeated almost annually and argues that this shows considerable resistance to their enforcement (*Problemas campesinos*, pp. 117–118).

57 Meyer, *Problemas campesinos*, p. 28; Frazer, "Desamortización," p. 623; Powell, *Liberalismo*, pp. 71–74; González Navarro, *Anatomía*, pp. 156–157. In one exception to this generalization, Luis de la Rosa proposed that the government give away lands in unpopulated areas to colonists. See his *Observaciones sobre varios puntos concernientes a la administración pública del estado de Zacatecas* (Baltimore: J. Murphy y Cía., 1851), pp. 9–13.

58 González y González, "El agrarismo liberal," p. 487; Hale, *Mexican Liberalism*, p. 257; Powell, *Liberalismo*, pp. 72, 81, 84–85; Frazer, "Desamortización," pp. 74–86; Reyes Heroles, *El liberalismo mexicano*, 2:539–626.

59 Andrés Molina Enriquez reprints the text of the law in his *Esbozo de la historia de los primeros diez años de la revolucíon agraria de México (de 1910*

a 1920), hecho a grandes rasgos, 5 vols., 2d ed. (Mexico: Museo Nacional de Antropología, Historia y Etnografía, 1937), 3:101–103. See also González Navarro, "Independencia," p. 168. Macune, *El estado de México*, pp. 145–151, emphasizes the jurisdictional struggle between radicals in the state and national governments. On Church wealth and confiscations from 1821 through 1855, see Jan Bazant, *Alienation of Church Wealth: Social and Economic Aspects of the Liberal Revolution, 1856–1875* (Cambridge: Cambridge University Press, 1971), pp. 14–39.

60   María de la Luz Parcero López, *Lorenzo de Zavala, fuente y orígen de la reforma liberal en México* (Mexico: INAH, 1969): 11, 12, 254, 257.

61   François Chevalier, "Survivances seigneuriales et présages de la révolution agraire dans le nord du Mexique (fin du xviie et xixe siècle)" *Revue Historique* 222 (1959): 1–18; Chevalier, "The North Mexican Hacienda," in *The New World Looks at Its History*, ed. Archibald R. Lewis and Thomas F. McGann (Austin: University of Texas Press, 1963), pp. 104–106.

62   Ibid.

63   Meyer, *Problemas campesinos*, pp. 36–38.

64   González Navarro, *Anatomía*, p. 161. Valadés, *Alamán* p. 476.

65   Frazer, "Desamortización," p. 626; González Navarro, *Anatomía*, pp. 161–162; Meyer, *Problemas campesinos*, pp. 40–59; Reyes Heroles, *El liberalismo mexicano*, 3:577–579.

66   Moisés González Navarro, "La venganza del Sur," *Historia mexicana* 21 (abril–junio 1972): 677–692; Meyer, *Problemas campesinos*, pp. 59–61; González Navarro, *Anatomía*, pp. 33, 43, 157; Leticia Reina, *Las rebeliones campesinas en México (1819–1906)* (Mexico: Siglo Veintiuno, 1980), pp. 85–120. Taking a more cynical view of Alvarez's motives is Díaz Díaz, *Caudillos y caciques*, who argues that the villagers gained little while Alvarez became a wealthy hacendado. The most recent and sophisticated analysis of the role of Alvarez and the peasantry in the South is Mallon, "Peasants and State Formation."

67   Meyer, *Problemas campesinos*, pp. 29–30; Frazer, "Desamortización," p. 623.

68   Moisés González Navarro, "Instituciones indígenas en México independiente," in *Métodos y resultados de la política indigenista en México. Memorias del Instituto Nacional Indigenista* 6 (1954): 147; Sims, *Descolonización*, pp. 18–20; Costeloe, *Primera república*, pp. 87–113.

69   Meyer, *Problemas campesinos*, pp. 9–10; González Navarro, "Instituciones indígenas," p. 147.

70   González Navarro, *Anatomía*, pp. 160, 161.

71   Meyer, *Problemas campesinos*, pp. 31, 103–115; Jean Meyer, "El ocaso

de Manuel Lozada," *Historia Mexicana* 18 (abril–junio 1969): 535–568; Evelyn Hu-DeHart, "Peasant Rebellion in the Northwest: The Yaqui Indians of Sonora, 1740–1976," in Friedrich Katz ed., *Riot, Rebellion, and Revolution: Rural Social Conflict in Mexico* (Princeton, N.J.: Princeton University Press, 1988), pp. 141–175.

72   González Navarro, *Pensamiento de Alamán*, p. 160; González Navarro, *Anatomía*, pp. 163–165; González Navarro, *Raza y tierra*, pp. 104–105.

73   Macune, *El Estado de México*, pp. 145–151. Following a different line of reasoning, Charles Hale concluded that "We are led to suggest, then, that federalism as a juridical form was not a distinguishing feature of Mexican liberalism." *Mexican Liberalism*, p. 85.

74   Sinkin, *The Liberal Reform*, pp. 55–74.

75   Brading, "Nationalism and Liberalism," pp. 154, 183.

76   Alamán, *Historia de México*, 5:712.

77   Hale, "The War with the United States," pp. 153–173; González Navarro, *Anatomía*, pp. 211–276; Frank Safford, "Politics, Ideology and Society in Post-Independence Spanish America," *The Cambridge History of Latin America*, v. 3, *From Independence to c. 1870* (Cambridge: Cambridge University Press), p. 398; Parkes, *A History of Mexico*, p. 262.

78   Their names, political classifications, and state of birth are listed in Appendix A.

79   For example, José María Yáñez fought against the centralists in 1833 and rebelled against Paredes and for federalism in 1846. He rebelled against Arista in 1852, was named secretaría de guerra y marina by Comonfort in 1856, but joined the conservatives during the War of the Reform, for which he was dismissed from the army when the liberals won. He fought against the French forces until the Regency was established when he accepted the position of jefe político of the department of Guanajuato under the Empire and later accepted membership in the Order of Guadalupe from Maximilian.

80   See chapter 5.

81   Stephen M. Stigler, *The History of Statistics: The Measurement of Uncertainty before 1900* (Cambridge, Mass.: Belknap Press of Harvard University Press, 1986), p. 28. On the historical development of the attitude that aggregates are a better guide than individual examples and observations, an idea which seems to have affected measurable numbers of historians only in the last several decades, see Theodore M. Porter, *The Rise of Statistical Thinking, 1820–1900* (Princeton, N.J.: Princeton University Press, 1986).

Four   Paths to Power

1   Hale, *Mexican Liberalism*, p. 115.

2   Alamán, *Historia de México*, 5:712, 851.

3   Sierra, *Political Evolution*, pp. 185–186, 203–204; Reyes Heroles, *El liberalismo mexicano*, 2:107–111; Chevalier, "Conservateurs et libéraux," pp. 457–474; Costeloe, *La primera república*, pp. 185–187, 438–439.

4   Sinkin, "The Mexican Constitutional Congress," pp. 2–3. See also his *The Mexican Reform*, pp. 31–54.

5   See the review essay by Elizabeth Kuznesof and Robert Oppenheimer, "The Family and Society in Nineteenth-Century Latin America: An Historiographical Introduction," *Journal of Family History* 10 (Fall 1985): 215–234. Diana Balmori, "The Family and Politics: Three Generations (1790–1890)," *Journal of Family History* 10 (Fall 1985): 247–257, concludes (p. 256), "In nineteenth-century Latin America political institutions were less important than families and many political structures were in fact the institutionalization of a dimension of family activity."

6   For general trends, see John E. Kicza, "The Role of the Family in Economic Development in Nineteenth-Century Latin America," *Journal of Family History* 10 (Fall 1985): 235–246. The risks of clear identification of family business with distinct political factions are evident from studies of families that did not diversify. The Martínez del Rio and the Sánchez Navarro families each suffered major losses when the liberals finally defeated the conservatives in the 1860s. See David W. Walker, *Kinship, Business, and Politics: The Martínez del Rio Family in Mexico, 1823–1867* (Austin: University of Texas Press, 1986), and Charles H. Harris III, *A Mexican Family Empire: The Latifundio of the Sánchez Navarros, 1765–1867* (Austin: University of Texas Press, 1975).

7   Wolf and Hansen, "Caudillo Politics," p. 176.

8   *Miners and Merchants*, p. 413. Justo Sierra, *Political Evolution*, p. 203, notes that "The rich, through selfishness or cowardice, were almost wholly withdrawn from public affairs, endlessly parroting in the drawing room, the manor, the sacristy, their favorite maxim: 'Only those who have nothing to lose can afford to take part in politics.'"

9   López Cámara, *La estructura económica y social*, p. 192. Others have argued that landowners lived in major population centers and left rural areas to the workers and administrators. See Reyes Heroles, *Liberalismo*, pp. 90–92, and Hale, *Mexican Liberalism*, p. 46.

10   "The Bases of Political Alignment in Early Republican Spanish Amer-

ica," in *New Approaches to Latin American History*, ed. Richard Graham and Peter H. Smith (Austin: University of Texas Press, 1974), p. 85. Others have argued that landowners were ubiquitous. See, for example, Jan Bazant, "Tres revoluciones mexicanas," *Historia mexicana* 10 (1960): 231. Hale, *Mexican Liberalism*, p. 181.

11   "Political Power and Landownership in Nineteenth Century Latin America," in *New Approaches to Latin American History*, pp. 134–135.

12   For descriptions of the statistics used in this chapter, see Appendix C.

13   These percentages are the sum of military officers (column two) and those who held both military rank and legal degrees (column three).

14   Points two and three have been made explicitly by Safford, "The Bases of Political Alignment," pp. 71–111.

15   For example, John E. Kicza suggests that in the late colonial period the "great families" had little use for education in the professions or military titles since they already enjoyed privileged access to wealth and power. *Colonial Entrepreneurs: Families and Business in Bourbon Mexico City* (Albuquerque: University of New Mexico Press, 1983), pp. 15, 28–30

16   John Kicza, for example, points out that sharing an occupation is not necessarily evidence of social similarity, that is, that economic stratification exists within professions as well as between them. See his *Colonial Entrepreneurs*, p. xv.

17   Details of this description are based on Juan de Dios Peza, "Entrada del Ejército Trigarante á México," in *Episodios históricos de la Guerra de Independencia* (Mexico: "El Tiempo," 1910), pp. 301–307. The quoted phrase appears on p. 302.

18   Frank N. Samponaro, "The Political Role of the Army in Mexico" (Ph.D. dissertation, State University of New York at Stony Brook, 1974), pp. 28–30.

19   Lucina Moreno Valle, "Poder Legislativo," in *Catálogo de la Colección Lafragua de la Biblioteca Nacional de México, 1821–1853*, Instituto de Investigaciones Bibliográficas, Biblioteca Nacional de México, Serie: Guías, no. 2 (Mexico: Universidad Nacional Autónoma de México, 1975), pp. 893–947; Francisco Zarco, *Historia del Congreso Extraordinario Constituyente [1856–1857]* (Mexico City: El Colegio de Mexico, 1956).

20   References for each state are listed in the initial sections of the bibliography.

Five   Holding on to Power

1   Cabinet instability is even more extreme if provisional holders of those positions are counted. The totals would be 77 ministers of war, 94 justice ministers, 85 foreign ministers, and 119 ministers of the treasury. A list of presidents and cabinet ministers as well as emperors and provisional juntas from 1821 to the present with the dates they entered and left office may be found in *Diccionario Porrúa de historia, biografía y geografía de México,* 5th ed., s.v. "Gobiernos de México independiente," and *Enciclopedia de México,* s.v. "Gabinetes." To simplify calculations, all terms were rounded to the nearest month.

2   The hypothesis that variations in background were a significant source of conflict will be examined below. See chapter 6.

3   For regional variation, see chapter 6 below. For political and military experience, see chapter 4 above.

4   The results presented in the following tables were calculated by subprogram ANOVA of SPSSX, release 3.0, using a classical experimental approach. Interaction effects were not included. See SPSS, Inc., *SPSSX: User's Guide,* pp. 450–463. For brief descriptions of statistics, see Appendix C.

5   Deleting provisional presidents and temporary cabinet officers from these analyses allows for more statistical consistency. A large part of the difference between provisional and permanent officeholders seems to be well accounted for by the intention with which the term began. Since we are more interested in social and political variation, it makes sense to eliminate this source of interference. In addition, the matrix must have fewer cells than cases, so it helps to reduce the number of categories. Finally, biographical data are more difficult to obtain for a larger number of those who served only provisionally, making their inclusion less desirable.

6   The grand mean in table 5.8 is higher than the mean in table 5.7 since those with shorter careers tended to have missing values for more of the relevant independent variables and were not included in the calculations.

7   See table 5.8.

8   Alamán, *Historia de México,* 5:918.

9   Compare the results of tables 5.5 and 5.6 with table 5.8.

Six   Social and Political Landscapes

1   Quoted by Hale, *Mexican Liberalism,* p. 105.

2   The best study of regional influences on political outlooks and out-

comes is Héctor Aguilar Camín, "The Relevant Tradition: Sonoran Leaders in the Revolution," in *Caudillo and Peasant in the Mexican Revolution*, ed. D. A. Brading (Cambridge: Cambridge University Press, 1980), pp. 92–123. Region has been an important consideration in many studies of Mexican history. Two classic works are Eric R. Wolf, "The Mexican Bajío in the Eighteenth Century," in *Synoptic Studies of Mexican Culture* (New Orleans: Middle American Research Institute, Tulane University, 1957), pp. 180–199; and Friedrich Katz, "Labor Conditions on Haciendas in Porfirian Mexico: Some Trends and Tendencies," *Hispanic American Historical Review* 54 (February 1974): 30–47. Several important regional studies appeared in the 1980s: Thomas Benjamin and William McNellie, eds., *Other Mexicos: Essays on Regional Mexican History, 1876–1911* (Albuquerque: University of New Mexico Press, [1984]); Brian R. Hamnett, *Roots of Insurgency: Mexican Regions, 1750–1824* (Cambridge: Cambridge University Press, [1986]); John Tutino, *From Insurrection to Revolution in Mexico: Social Bases of Agrarian Violence, 1750–1940* (Princeton, N.J.: Princeton University Press, [1986]).

3   Parkes, *A History of Mexico*, p. 180.

4   For example, "Geographically it was a war of the outside against the center." Priestly, *The Mexican Nation*, pp. 337–338. More recently, "From the outset, the country split into factions: the conservative core—the states of Puebla, México, and Querétaro—against the peripheral areas where liberals were traditionally strong." Bazant, *Concise History*, p. 77.

5   Chevalier, "Conservateurs et libéraux," pp. 457–474.

6   Brading, "Nationalism and Liberalism," p. 185. Sinkin, *The Mexican Reform*, pp. 37–39, supports this view of Reform era liberals. For a more recent and sophisticated elaboration of the connections between region and politics, see Safford, "Politics, Ideology, and Society," pp. 404–409.

7   Brading, "Nationalism and Liberalism," p. 186. See also Tutino, *From Insurrection to Revolution*, pp. 142–182, 215–241.

8   Brading suggested that it would take "a generation of research to discover the distribution of political power in each region and to ascertain from which elements in society local leaders drew their support." Brading, "Nationalism and Liberalism," p. 184. Almost two decades later, this still applies.

9   D. A. Brading, *Haciendas and Ranchos in the Mexican Bajío: León, 1700–1860* (Cambridge: Cambridge University Press, 1978). Two of the best regional studies for this period concern the far North: Voss, *On the Periphery*; Weber, *The Mexican Frontier*.

10   Parkes, *History of Mexico*, p. 180.

11   Putnam, *Comparative Study*, p. 18.

12   For example, Lucas Alamán, probably the most famous conservative, came from a prominent and wealthy family and was paid to defend the economic interests of the heirs of Cortés.

13   For example, D. A. Brading, *Miners and Merchants in Bourbon Mexico, 1763–1810* (Cambridge: Cambridge University Press, 1971); Walker, *Kinship, Business and Politics*.

14   The exception is Manuel Gutiérrez Zamora who served as governor of the state of Veracruz beginning in 1856.

15   In ambiguous or controversial cases the last position taken while holding office as a cabinet minister or president was used to determine the political category. A substantial minority of cabinet officials (especially those who were less well-known or who served only briefly) remain undetermined. On the classification process, see chapter 3.

16   Parkes, *A History of Mexico*, p. 180; Brading, "Nationalism and Liberalism," p. 185.

17   On socialization and political factionalism, see chapter 4.

18   The definition of "North" that I use here is that area north of the canyons of the Moctezuma and Santiago rivers where few settled Indians lived before the conquest and where there had been few *encomiendas*. Simpson, *Many Mexicos*, pp. vii–viii, 159–160.

19   Practical considerations of distance meant that militia duty in the North was less likely to lead to service in the army. Weber, *The Mexican Frontier*, pp. 118–119.

20   "Taking local variations into account, it seems clear that . . . northern Mexico's political institutions were becoming more representative, its economic structure more capitalistic, its settlers more independent from the Church and the military." Weber, *The Mexican Frontier*, p. 282. Voss's *On the Periphery* is an outstanding study of the local variation in Sinaloa and Sonora. See also Katz, "Labor Conditions on Haciendas." For a contrasting view, Frank Safford has written that "liberalism was a dominant force in such states as Zacatecas, Michoacán or Jalisco; [but] it was less characteristic of the sparsely populated far north of Mexico which was more removed from national politics and where a few large landowners could dominate politics." Safford, "Politics, Ideology and Society in Post-Independence Spanish America," p. 407. A good illustration of this possibility is Harris, *A Mexican Family Empire*. The debate on the North is analyzed by David J. Weber, "Turner, the Boltonians, and the Borderlands," *American Historical Review* 91 (February 1986): 66–81.

21   William B. Taylor, *Landlord and Peasant in Colonial Oaxaca* (Stanford,

Calif.: Stanford University Press, 1972), passim; Brian R. Hamnett, *Politics and Trade in Southern Mexico, 1750–1821* (London: Cambridge University Press, 1971). Taylor, *Drinking, Homocide, and Rebellion in Colonial Mexican Villages* (Stanford, Calif.: Stanford University Press, 1979), compares villages in Oaxaca with those of central Mexico and finds less Spanish influence in Oaxaca.

22 Friedrich Katz, "Rural Uprisings in Preconquest and Colonial Mexico," in *Riot, Rebellion, and Revolution: Rural Social Conflict in Mexico*, ed. Katz (Princeton, N.J.: Princeton University Press, 1988), pp. 88–92.

23 Otero, *Ensayo*, pp. 50–51.

24 Reyes Heroles, *Liberalismo*, pp. 90–92; Hale, *Mexican Liberalism*, p. 46.

25 Safford, "Bases of Political Alignment," pp. 108–109.

26 Powell, *Liberalismo*, pp. 69–70; Charles R. Berry, *The Reform in Oaxaca, 1856–1876: A Microhistory of the Liberal Revolution* (Lincoln: University of Nebraska Press, 1981). For some pre-Reforma era attempts to alter the distribution of property in the countryside, see chapter 3.

27 Those born in rural areas include such prominent radicals as Juan Alvarez, Manuel Doblado, Francisco García Salinas, Jesús González Ortega, Benito Juárez, Melchor Ocampo, Manuel Crescencio Rejón, and Ignacio Zaragoza.

Seven   Conditions and Convictions

1 Padrón Municipalidad de México (1848). Archivo del Antiguo Ayuntamiento (Mexico City), v. 3408–3409.

2 Of the 229 individuals I have been able to categorize on the basis of their politics, thirty-three were known to have died before the 1848 census was taken. The fifty-two who appear in the census are listed in Appendix B. The census usually lists the address, portion of the dwelling occupied, the names of heads of household and residents, age, marital status, origin, occupation, length of residence, rent paid or value of the property if the resident is the owner, and the name of the owner of the property. Some of those enumerating the census consistently failed to note some of the information, especially the names or numbers of residents other than the head of household.

3 The remainder of the biographical information included in these sketches is taken principally from *Diccionario Porrúa de historia, biografía y geografía de México*, 5th ed. The examples consist of the three households with fewest servants and the three households with the most servants.

4 For Latin America, see Kuznesof and Oppenheimer, "The Family and Society," pp. 215–234, and the works cited therein. For England, see the essays by Peter Laslett, Richard Wall, and W. A. Armstrong, in Laslett, ed., *Household and Family in Past Time* (Cambridge: Cambridge University Press, 1972), especially pp. 126, 154, 207.

5 The results presented in the following tables were calculated by subprogram ANOVA of SPSSX, release 2.1, using a classical experimental approach. Interaction effects were not statistically significant. See Appendix C.

6 Silvia M. Arrom, *The Women of Mexico City, 1790–1857* (Stanford, Calif.: Stanford University Press, 1985), p. 7.

7 Of these six, two were conservatives, two were moderates, one was radical, and one I have not been able to classify. See Appendix B.

8 Forty-six of fifty-two lived in the 1st, 3rd, 5th, 7th, 9th, 13, and 14th *cuarteles*. The rents of those six who lived farther from the Zocalo averaged $43, about the same as the overall average. See Appendix B. Although the edge of the city was partially inhabited by Indians living in shacks, there were substantial houses for the elite. The first Spanish ambassador to Mexico, for example, settled in a house north of the Alameda park. See Frances Calderón de la Barca, *Life in Mexico: The Letters of Fanny Calderón de la Barca, with New Material from the Author's Private Journals*, edited and annotated by Howard T. Fisher and Marion Hall Fisher (New York: Doubleday, 1966), p. 697, n. 2.

9 Sonia Lombardo de Ruiz, "Construction and Contractors: A Methodological Approach to the Study of Architectural Styles in Mexico City, 1780–1805," *Latin American Research Review* 10 (1975): 128–129; Alejandra Moreno Toscano and Carlos Aguirre Anaya, "Migrations to Mexico City in the Nineteenth Century: Research Approaches," *Journal of International Studies and World Affairs* 17 (1975): 27–42.

10 The comments on the costs of housing do not appear in all published versions of her letters, but were part of the tenth letter, written 25 February 1840. The most convenient edition of the work containing these lines is *Life in Mexico* (Berkeley: University of California Press, 1982), p. 101. The edition most frequently cited by historians, *Life in Mexico*, edited and annotated by Fisher and Fisher, does not contain this material.

11 *Life in Mexico* (Berkeley: University of California Press, 1982), p. 509.

12 The role of the family in distributing economic resources is well-known. On kinship and housing choices, see Linda Greenow, "Microgeographic Analysis as an Index to Family Structure and Networks," *Journal of Family History* 10 (1985): 278–279.

Eight   Origins of Instability in Mexico

1   González Navarro, *Anatomía del poder*, pp. 1–2. For an example of the
continuing influence of Santa Anna over the history of Mexico, see the
recent work of David Bushnell and Neill Macaulay, *The Emergence of
Latin America in the Nineteenth Century* (New York: Oxford University
Press, 1988), pp. 71–82, which begins: "The career of Antonio López
de Santa Anna represents one of the more conspicuous stumbling
blocks in the way of those who would explain nineteenth-century Latin
America's political divisions as the manifestation of underlying divisions between socioeconomic groups whose views and interests were
supposedly best represented by either liberal or conservative parties."
This is not the place to engage those who would use Santa Anna
as a refutation of any general interpretation of Mexico's early republican political history. The available literature on Santa Anna is already
voluminous in comparison to other themes. To allow the discussion
of early republican Mexico to continue to revolve around the role of
Santa Anna is to concede the argument in favor of his significance
before another position is developed. I think it would be possible to
make the argument that during his alliances with diverse political factions, Santa Anna remained a consistent militarist and continually
defended the interests of the national army even if it meant expropri-
ating or threatening the Church. This gave Santa Anna common
ground with conservatives who favored a strong national army and
liberals who wanted to weaken the Church. This may not be the sort
of ideological consistency that some would require, but it is a perpet-
ual position. Santa Anna's association with the state of Veracruz, a
liberal stronghold in the view of most historians, has puzzled many as
well. But as this study shows, the state of Veracruz produced a large
number of conservative politicians of national reputation as well. The
local economic and social contradictions may have facilitated Santa
Anna's alterations between radicals, moderates, and conservatives. The
economic interests of Veracruz included importers as well as growers
of cotton, manufacturers as well as importers of textiles, tobacco farmers and importers who were alternately dealt prosperity or ruin depending on the government's view of the tobacco monopoly.

2   Compared to the Sonoran revolutionaries studied by Héctor Aguilar
Camín, these nineteenth-century radicals seem to have been notably
less hostile to their social and economic superiors. Perhaps their liberal ideology allowed them to focus on the obstacles posed by corporate property and left a greater respect for the private property of their
political foes than prevailed in Sonora during the Revolution. See
Aguilar Camín, "The Relevant Tradition."

Bibliography

Archival Material

Padrón Municipalidad de México (1848). Archivo del Antiguo Ayuntamiento. v. 3408–3409. Mexico City.

Bibliographies

Iguíniz, Juan B. *Bibliografía biográfica mexicana*. Mexico: Universidad Nacional Autónoma de México, 1969.

Mundo Lo, Sara de. *Index to Spanish American Collective Biography. Vol. 2: Mexico*. Boston: G. K. Hall, [1982].

Collective Biographies

Presidents and Cabinet Ministers

Diccionario Porrúa de historia, biografía y geografía de México, 5th ed.

Enciclopedia de México, 1967–1976.

García Purón, Manuel. *México y sus gobernantes: biografías*. Mexico: Porrúa, 1964.

Leduc, Alberto, Luis Lara y Pardo, and Carlos Roumagnac. *Diccionario de geografía, historia y biografía mexicanas*. Paris: Librería de la Vda. de Ch. Bouret, 1910.

Paz, Ireneo. *Los hombres prominentes de México*. Mexico: "La Patria," 1888.

Sierra, Carlos J. *Historia de la administración hacendaria en México, 1821–1970*. Mexico: Secretaría de Hacienda y Crédito Público, 1970.

Sierra Domínguez, Sergio, and Roberto Martínez Barreda, comps. *México y sus funcionarios*. Mexico: Cárdenas, 1959.

Sosa, Francisco. *Biografías de mexicanos distinguidos*. Mexico: Secretaría de Fomento, 1884.

——. *Efemérides históricas y biográficas*. 2 vols. Mexico: G. A. Esteva, 1883.

Insurgents

Amador, Elías. *Noticias biográficas de insurgentes apodados*. Mexico: Secretaría de Educación Pública, 1946.

Miquel i Vergés, José María. *Diccionario de insurgentes*. 2d ed. Mexico: Porrúa, 1980.

Villaseñor y Villaseñor, Alejandro. *Biografías de los héroes y caudillos de la independencia*. 2d ed. 2 vols. Mexico: Editorial Jus, 1962.

Military Officers

Carreño, Alberto M. *Jefes del Ejército mexicano en 1847. Biografías de generales de división y de brigada y de coroneles del Ejército mexicano por fines del año del 1847. Manuscrito anónimo, adicionado en gran parte y precedido de un estudio acerca la participación del Ejército en la vida política de México durante la primera mitad del siglo xix, con numeroso documentos inéditos. . . .* Mexico: Secretaría de Fomento, 1914.

National Legislators

Moreno Valle, Lucina. "Poder Legislativo." In *Catálogo de la Colección Lafragua de la Biblioteca Nacional de México, 1821–1853*, pp. 893–947. Instituto de Investigaciones Bibliográficas, Biblioteca Nacional de México, Serie: Guías, no. 2. Mexico: Universidad Nacional Autónoma de México, 1975.

Zarco, Francisco. *Historia del Congreso Extraordinario Constituyente [1856–1857]*. Mexico, 1857–1861; reprint ed., Mexico: El Colegio de México, 1956.

State Governors

Alta California

Weber, David J. *The Mexican Frontier, 1821–1846: The American Southwest under Mexico*. Albuquerque: University of New Mexico Press, 1982.

Aguascalientes

Bernal Sánchez, Jesús. *Apuntes históricos, geográficos y estadísticos del Estado de Aguascalientes*. Aguascalientes: Alberto E. Pedroza, 1928.

Chiapas

García Soto, J. Mario. *Geografía general de Chiapas*. Mexico: n.p., 1969.

Chihuahua

Almada, Francisco R. *Gobernantes de Chihuahua*. Chihuahua: Talleres Gráficos del Gobierno del Estado, 1929.

Coahuila

Alessio Robles, Vito. *Coahuila y Téjas, desde la consumación de la independencia hasta el tratado de Guadalupe Hidalgo*. 2 vols. Mexico: n.p., 1945–1946.

Rodríguez González, José. *Geografía del Estado de Coahuila*. Mexico: Sociedad de Edición y Librería Franco-Americana, 1926.

Distrito Federal

Puig Casauranc, José Manuel. *Atlas general del Distrito Federal*. Mexico: n.p., 1930.

Durango

Diccionario ilustrado y enciclopedia general del Estado de Durango. Mexico: Fernández Editores, 1974.

Guanajuato

Rodríguez Fausto, Jesús. *Guía de gobernantes de Guanajuato*. Guanajuato: Universidad de Guanajuato, Archivo Histórico, 1965.

Guerrero

Diccionario ilustrado y enciclopedia general del Estado de Guerrero. Mexico: Fernández Editores, 1974.

Jalisco

Cambre, Manuel. *Gobiernos y gobernadores de Jalisco, desde la declaración de independencia de Nueva Galicia hasta el día*. Guadalajara: Escuela de Artes y Oficios del Estado, 1910.

"Fuentes documentales: cronología de los gobernantes del Estado de Jalisco." *Memorias de la Academia Mexicana de la Historia Correspondiente de la Real de Madrid* 20 (julio–septiembre 1961): 303–324.

México

Venegas, Aurelio J. *Indice cronológico de los gobernantes del estado de México y de los benemeritos y ciudadanos del mismo*. Toluca: Talleres de la Escuela de Artes, 1912.

Michoacán

Aguilar Ferreira, Melesio. *Los Gobernadores de Michoacán*. Morelia: n.p., 1950.

Bravo Ugarte, José. *Historia sucinta de Michoacán*. 3 vols. Mexico: Editorial Jus, 1964.

Romero Flores, Jesús. *Geografía del Estado de Michoacán*. Morelia: Talleres Tipográficos de la E.T.I. "Alvaro Obregón," 1928.

Nuevo León

Diccionario ilustrado y enciclopedia regional del Estado de Nuevo León. Mexico: Fernández Editores, 1969.

Nuevo México
Weber, David J. *The Mexican Frontier, 1821–1846: The American Southwest under Mexico.* Albuquerque: University of New Mexico Press, 1982.

Oaxaca
Báez, Victoriano D. *Compendio de historia de Oaxaca.* Oaxaca: Julián S. Soto, 1909.

Taracena, Angel. *Efemerides oaxaqueños.* Oaxaca: n.p., 1941.

Puebla
Gómez Haro, Eduardo. *Puebla y sus gobernadores.* Puebla: Negociacíon, 1915.

Palacios, Enrique Juan. "Puebla; su territorio y sus habitantes." *Memorias de la Sociedad Científica "Antonio Alzate"* 36 (1916): 1–716.

Querétaro
Frías, Valentín F. "Gobernantes de Querétaro del 27 de junio del 1821 al 27 de junio de 1921." *Memorias de la Sociedad Científica "Antonio Alzate"* 40 (1922): 591–600.

San Luis Potosí
Grimaldo, Isaac. *Gobernantes potosinos, 1590–1939.* San Luis Potosí: Tip. Esc. "Hijos del Ejército No. 10," 1939.

Sinaloa
Olea, Héctor R. "Gobernantes del Estado de Sinaloa." In *Estudios históricos de Sinaloa,* pp. 373–407. Mexico: Congreso Mexicana de Historia, 1960.

Sonora
Almada, Francisco R. *Diccionario de historia, geografía y biografía sonorenses.* Chihuahua: [Impresora Ruiz Sandoval, 1952].

Tabasco
Bulnes, Pepe. *La agenda tabasqueña.* [Mexico: n.p., 1955].

Mestre Ghigliazza, Manuel. *Apuntes para una relación cronológica de los gobernantes de Tabasco.* Mérida: Carlos R. Menéndez, 1934.

Tamaulipas
Covían Martínez, Vidal. "Los gobernantes de Tamaulipas." *Cuadernos de Historia* 1 (febrero 1968): 80–84.

Zorrilla, Juan Fidel. *Historia de Tamaulipas.* 2d ed. Mexico: Editorial Jus, 1977.

Veracruz
Melgarejo Vivanco, José Luis. *Breve historia de Veracruz.* Jalapa: Biblioteca de la Facultad de Filosofía y Letras, Universidad Veracruzana, [1960].

Diccionario ilustrado y enciclopedia regional de Veracruz. Mexico: Fernández Editores, 1973.

Yucatán
Bolio, Edmundo. *Diccionario histórico, geográfico y biográfico de Yucatán.*

Mexico: I.C.D., 1944.

Orosa Díaz, Jaime. *Yucatán, panorama histórico, geográfico y cultural.* Mexico: Secretaría de Educación Pública, 1945.

Zacatecas

Rodríguez Flores, Emilio. *Compendio histórico de Zacatecas.* 2d ed. N.P.: Benito Juárez, 1977.

Other Works Cited

Aguilar Camín, Héctor. "The Relevant Tradition: Sonoran Leaders in the Revolution." In *Caudillo and Peasant in the Mexican Revolution,* pp. 92–123. Edited by D. A. Brading. Cambridge: Cambridge University Press, 1980.

Alamán, Lucas. *Historia de México desde los primeros movimientos que prepararon su independencia en el año de 1808 hasta la época presente.* 5 vols. Mexico: J. Mariano Lara, 1850; facsimile ed., Mexico: Fondo de Cultura Económica, 1985.

Anna, Timothy. *The Fall of the Royal Government in Mexico City.* Lincoln: University of Nebraska Press, 1978.

———. "The Finances of Mexico City during the War of Independence." *Journal of Latin American Studies* 4 (May 1972): 55–75.

———. *Spain & the Loss of America.* Lincoln: University of Nebraska Press, [1983].

Archer, Christon I. *The Army in Bourbon Mexico, 1760–1810.* Albuquerque: University of New Mexico Press, 1977.

———. "Pardos, Indians, and the Army of New Spain: Inter-relationships and Conflicts, 1780–1810. *Journal of Latin American Studies* 6 (November 1974): 231–255.

Ardant, Gabriel. "Financial Policy and Economic Infrastructure of Modern States and Nations." In *The Formation of National States in Western Europe,* pp. 164–242. Edited by Charles Tilly. Princeton, N.J.: Princeton University Press, 1975.

Arrangoiz y Berzábel, Francisco de Paula de. *México desde 1808 hasta 1867.* 4 vols. Madrid: Imprenta a cargo de Estrada, 1871–1872.

Arrom, Silvia M. "Popular Politics in Mexico City: The Parián Riot, 1828." *Hispanic American Historial Review* 68 (May 1988): 245–268.

———. *The Women of Mexico City, 1790–1857.* Stanford, Calif.: Stanford University Press, 1985.

Aya, Rod. "Theories of Revolution Reconsidered." *Theory and Society* 8 (1979): 39–99.

Balmori, Diana. "The Family and Politics: Three Generations (1790–1890)." *Journal of Family History* 10 (Fall 1985): 247–257.

Bazant, Jan. *Alienation of Church Wealth: Social and Economic Aspects of the Liberal Revolution, 1856–1875*. Cambridge: Cambridge University Press, 1971.

———. *A Concise History of Mexico from Hidalgo to Cardenas, 1805–1940*. Cambridge: Cambridge University Press, 1977.

———. *Historia de la deuda exterior de México, 1823–1946*. Foreword by Antonio Ortiz Mena. Mexico: El Colegio de México, [1968].

———. "Tres revoluciones mexicanas." *Historia mexicana* 10 (1960): 220–242.

Beezley, William H. "Caudillismo: An Interpretive Note." *Journal of Inter-American Studies* 11 (July 1969): 345–352.

Benjamin, Thomas, and William McNellie, eds. *Other Mexicos: Essays on Regional Mexican History, 1876–1911*. Albuquerque: University of New Mexico Press, [1984].

Benson, Nettie Lee. "The Contested Mexican Election of 1812." *Hispanic American Historical Review* 26 (August 1946): 339–350.

———. *La diputación provincial y el federalismo mexicano*. Mexico: El Colegio de México, 1955.

———. "The Plan of Casa Mata." *Hispanic American Historical Review* 25 (February 1945): 45–56.

———, ed. *Mexico and the Spanish Cortes, 1810–1822*. Austin: University of Texas Press, [1966].

Berge, Dennis E. "A Mexican Dilemma: The Mexico City Ayuntamiento and the Question of Loyalty, 1848." *Hispanic American Historical Review* 50 (May 1970): 229–256.

Berry, Charles R. *The Reform in Oaxaca, 1856–1876: A Microhistory of the Liberal Revolution*. Lincoln: University of Nebraska Press, 1981.

Blalock, Hubert M. *Social Statistics*. New York: McGraw-Hill, 1972.

Bottomore, T. B. *Elites and Society*. London: C. A. Watts, 1964.

Brading, David A. "Creole Nationalism and Mexican Liberalism." *Journal of Interamerican Studies and World Affairs* 15 (May 1973): 139–190.

———. "Government and Elite in Late Colonial Mexico." *Hispanic American Historical Review* 53 (August 1973): 389–414.

———. *Haciendas and Ranchos in the Mexican Bajío: León, 1700–1860*. Cambridge: Cambridge University Press, 1978.

———. *Miners and Merchants in Bourbon Mexico, 1763–1810*. Cambridge: Cambridge University Press, 1971.

———. *The Origins of Mexican Nationalism*. Cambridge: Centre of Latin American Studies, University of Cambridge, 1985.

Braun, Rudolph. "Taxation, Sociopolitical Structure and State-Building in Great Britain and Brandenberg-Prussia." In *The Formation of National States in Western Europe*, pp. 242–327. Edited by Charles Tilly.

Princeton, N.J.: Princeton University Press, 1975.

Broussard, Ray F. "The Mexican Liberals and the Curbing of the Military's Powers: Success or Failure?" *Annals of the Southeastern Conference on Latin American Studies* 10 (March 1979): 5–14.

Burkholder, M. A., and D. S. Chandler. "Creole Appointments and the Sale of Audiencia Positions in the Spanish Empire under the Early Bourbons, 1701–1750." *Journal of Latin American Studies* 4 (November 1972): 187–206.

————. *From Impotence to Authority: The Spanish Crown and the American Audiencias, 1687–1808.* Columbia: University of Missouri Press, 1977.

Bushnell, David, and Neill Macaulay. *The Emergence of Latin America in the Nineteenth Century.* New York: Oxford University Press, 1988.

Bustamante, Carlos María. *Apuntes para la historia del gobierno de general D. Antonio López de Santa Anna, 1841–1844.* Mexico: J. M. Lara, 1845.

————. *El gabinete mexicano durante el Segundo período de la administración del exmo. señor presidente D. Anastasio Bustamante, hasta la entrega del mando al exmo. señor presidente interino D. Antonio López de Santa Anna . . . .* 2 vols. Mexico: J. M. Lara, 1842.

Bwy, Douglas P. "Dimensions of Social Conflict in Latin America." In *When Men Revolt, and Why,* pp. 274–291. Edited by James Chowning Davies. New York: The Free Press, 1971.

————. "Political Instability in Latin America: The Cross-cultural Test of a Causal Model." *Latin American Research Review* 3 (Spring 1968): 17–66.

Calderón de la Barca, Frances. *Life in Mexico.* Berkeley: University of California Press, 1982.

————. *Life in Mexico: The Letters of Fanny Calderón de la Barca, with New Material from the Author's Private Journals* edited and annotated by Howard T. Fisher and Marion Hall Fisher. New York: Doubleday, 1966.

Callcott, Wilfred Hardy. *Santa Anna: The Story of an Enigma Who Once Was Mexico.* Norman: University of Oklahoma Press, 1936.

Carmagnani, Marcello. "Finanzas y estado en Mexico, 1820–1880," *Ibero-Amerikanisches Archiv* N.F. 9:3/4 (1983): 279–318.

Carvalho, Jose Murilo de. "Political Elites and State Building: The Case of Nineteenth Century Brazil." *Comparative Studies in Society and History* 24 (July 1982): 378–399.

Chevalier, François. "Conservateurs et libéraux au Mexique: Essai du sociologie et géographie politiques de l'indépendance a l'intervention française." *Cahiers d'Histoire Mondiale* 8 (1964): 457–474.

————. "The North Mexican Hacienda." In *The New World Looks at Its History,* pp. 95–107. Edited by Archibald R. Lewis and Thomas F.

McGann. Austin: University of Texas Press, 1963.

———. "Survivances seigneuriales et présages de la révolution agraire dans le nord du Mexique (fin du xviiiᵉ et xixᵉ siècle)." *Revue Historique* 222 (1959): 1–18.

Coatsworth, John H. "The Limits of Colonial Absolutism: The State in Eighteenth Century Mexico." In *Essays in the Political, Economic and Social History of Colonial Latin America*, pp. 25–51. Edited by Karen Spaulding. Newark: University of Delaware Press, 1982.

———. "Obstacles to Economic Growth in Nineteenth Century Mexico." *American Historical Review* 83 (February 1978): 80–100.

Conklin, John G. "Elite Studies: The Case of the Mexican Presidency." *Journal of Latin American Studies* 5 (November 1973): 247–269.

Cordero y Torres, Enrique. *Historia compendiada del Estado de Puebla.* 3 vols. [Mexico]: Grupo Literario "Bohemia Poblana," [1965–1966].

Costeloe, Michael P. "The Administration, Collection and Distribution of Tithes in the Archbishopric of Mexico, 1810–1860." *The Americas* 23 (July 1966): 3–27.

———. *Church and State in Independent Mexico—A Study of the Patronage Debate, 1821–1857.* London: Royal Historical Society, 1978.

———. Church-State Financial Negotiations in Mexico during the American War, 1846–1847." *Revista de historia de América* 60 (julio–diciembre 1965): 91–123.

———. *Church Wealth in Mexico: A Study of the "Juzgado de Capellanías" in the Archbishopric of Mexico, 1800–1856.* Cambridge: Cambridge University Press, 1967.

———. "Guadalupe Victoria and a Personal Loan from the Church in Independent Mexico." *The America* 25 (January 1969): 223–246.

———. "The Mexican Church in the Rebellion of the Polkos." *Hispanic American Historical Review* 46 (May 1966): 170–178.

———. *La primera república federal en México (1824–1835): (un estudio de los partidos políticos en el Mexico independiente).* Mexico: Fonda de Cultura Económica, 1975.

———. "A Pronunciamiento in Nineteenth-Century Mexico: '15 de julio de 1840.'" *Mexican Studies/Estudios Mexicanos* 4 (Summer 1988): 245–264.

———. "Santa Anna and the Gómez-Farías Regime in Mexico, 1833–1834." *The Americas* 31 (July 1974): 18–50.

———. "The Triangular Revolt in Mexico and the Fall of Anastasio Bustamante, August-October 1841." *Journal of Latin American Studies* 20 (1980): 337–360.

Cue Canovas, Agustín. *Historia social y económica de México, 1521–1854.* Mexico: F. Trillas, 1967.

Cuevas, Mariano. *Historia de la Nación mexicana*. Mexico: Talleres Tipográficos Modelo, 1940.

Cumberland, Charles C. *Mexico: The Struggle for Modernity*. New York: Oxford University Press, 1968.

Davies, James C. "Towards a Theory of Revolution." *American Sociological Review* 27 (February 1962): 5–19.

Dealy, Glen Caudill. *The Public Man: An Interpretation of Latin American and Other Catholic Countries*. Amherst: University of Massachusetts Press, 1977.

Dean, Warren. "Latin American *Golpes* and Economic Fluctuations, 1823–1966." *Social Science Quarterly* 51 (June 1970): 70–80.

Díaz Díaz, Fernando. *Caudillos y caciques: Antonio López de Santa Anna y Juan Alvarez*. Mexico: El Colegio de México, 1972.

Di Tella, Torcuato S. "The Dangerous Classes in Early Nineteenth Century Mexico." *Journal of Latin American Studies* 5 (May 1973): 79–105.

Dollar, Charles M., and Richard J. Jensen. *Historian's Guide to Statistics: Quantitative Analysis and Historical Research*. New York: Holt, Rinehart & Winston, 1971.

Dominguez, Jorge I. *Insurrection or Loyalty: The Breakdown of the Spanish American Empire*. Cambridge, Mass.: Harvard University Press, 1980.

Dowding, Keith M., and Richard Kimber. "The Meaning and Use of 'Political Stability.'" *European Journal of Political Research* 11 (September 1983): 229–243.

Farriss, N[ancy] M. *Crown and Clergy in Colonial Mexico, 1759–1821: The Crisis of Ecclesiastical Privilege*. London: Athalone Press, 1968.

Feierabend, Ivo K., and Rosalind L. Feierabend. "Aggressive Behaviors within Politics, 1948–1962: A Cross-National Study." *Journal of Conflict Resolution* 10 (September 1966): 249–271.

Feierabend, Ivo K.; Rosalind L. Feierabend; and Betty A. Nesvold. "Social Change and Political Violence: Cross-national Patterns." In *Violence in America*, pp. 606–668. Edited by Hugh Davis Graham and Ted Robert Gurr. New York: Signet Books, 1969.

Feierabend, Ivo K.; Rosalind L. Feierabend; and Ted Robert Gurr, eds. *Anger, Violence, and Politics: Theories and Research*. Englewood Cliffs, N.J.: Prentice-Hall, 1972.

Flores Caballero, Romeo. *Counterrevolution: The Role of the Spaniards in the Independence of Mexico, 1804–1838*. Translated by Jaime E. Rodríguez O. Lincoln: University of Nebraska Press, 1974.

———. "Del libre cambio al proteccionismo." *Historia mexicana* 19 (abril–junio 1970): 492–512.

Formación y desarrollo de la burgesía en México. Siglo xix. Introduction by Ciro F. S. Cardoso. Mexico: Siglo Veintiuno Editores, 1978.

Frazer, Donald J. "La política de desamortización en las comunidades indígenas—1856–1872." *Historia mexicana* 21 (abril–junio 1972): 615–652.

García, Genaro, gen. ed. *Documentos inéditos ó muy raros para la historia de México.* 36 vols. Mexico: Librería de la Vda. de Ch. Bouret, 1905–1911.

González Navarro, Moisés. *Anatomía del poder en México, 1848–1853.* Mexico: El Colegio de México, 1977.

——. "La independencia, el yorkinato y la libertad." In *Extremos de México: Homenaje a Don Daniel Cosío Villegas,* pp. 151–180. Mexico: El Colegio de México, 1971.

——. "Instituciones indígenas en México independiente." In *Métodos y resultados de la política indigenista en México. Memorias del Instituto Nacional Indigenista* 6 (1954): 113–169.

——. *El pensamiento político de Lucas Alamán.* Mexico: El Colegio de México, 1952).

——. "La venganza del Sur." *Historia mexicana* 21 (abril–junio 1972): 677–692.

González y González, Luis. "El agrarismo liberal." *Historia mexicana* 7 (abril–junio 1958): 469–496.

Graham, Richard. "Political Power and Landownership in Nineteenth-century Latin America." In *New Approaches to Latin American History,* pp. 112–136. Edited by Richard Graham and Peter H. Smith. Austin: University of Texas Press, 1974.

Green, Stanley C. *The Mexican Republic: The First Decade, 1823–1832.* Pittsburgh: University of Pittsburgh Press, 1987)

Greenow, Linda. "Microgeographic Analysis as an Index to Family Structure and Networks." *Journal of Family History* 10 (1985): 272–283.

Hale, Charles A. *Mexican Liberalism in the Age of Mora, 1821–1853.* New Haven, Conn.: Yale University Press, 1968.

——. "The Reconstruction of 19th Century Politics in Spanish America: A Case for the History of Ideas." *Latin American Research Review* 8 (Summer 1973): 53–73.

——. "The War with the United States and the Crisis in Mexican Thought." *The Americas* 14 (October 1957): 153–173.

Hamill, Hugh M., Jr. *The Hidalgo Revolt: Prelude to Mexican Independence.* Gainesville: University of Florida Press, 1966.

——. "Royalist Counterinsurgency in the Mexican War for Independence: The Lessons of 1811." *Hispanic American Historical Review* 53 (August 1973): 470–489.

——. "Was the Mexican Independence Movement a Revolution?" In *Dos revoluciones: México y los Estados Unidos.* Edición especial para El

Colegio de México y la American Historical Association. Mexico: Fomento Cultural Banamex, A.C., 1976.

Hamnett, Brian. "The Appropriation of Mexican Church Wealth by the Spanish Bourbon Government: The 'Consolidación de vales reales,' 1805–1809." *Journal of Latin American Studies* 1 (November 1969): 85–113.

———. "The Economic and Social Dimension of the Revolution of Independence in Mexico, 1800–1824." *Ibero-Amerikanisches Archiv* n.s., 6 (1980): 1–27.

———. "Mercantile Rivalry and Peninsular Division: The Consulados of New Spain and the Impact of the Bourbon Reforms." *Ibero-Amerikanisches Archiv* n.s., 2 (1976): 273–305.

———. "Mexico's Royalist Coalition: The Response to Revolution." *Journal of Latin American Studies* 12 (May 1980): 55–86.

———. "Obstáculos a la política agraria del despotismo ilustrado." *Historia mexicana* 20 (julio–septiembre 1976): 55–75.

———. *Politics and Trade in Southern Mexico, 1750–1821*. London: Cambridge University Press, 1971.

———. *Roots of Insurgency: Mexican Regions, 1750–1824*. Cambridge: Cambridge University Press, [1986].

Harris, Charles H., III. *A Mexican Family Empire: The Latifundio of the Sánchez Navarros, 1765–1867*. Austin: University of Texas Press, 1975.

Herrera Canales, Inés. *El comercio exterior de México, 1821–1975*. Mexico: El Colegio de México, 1977.

Hindricks, Harley H. "Determinants of Government Revenue Shares Among Less-developed Countries." *Economic Journal* 75 (September 1965): 546–556.

Hu-Dehart, Evelyn. "Peasant Rebellion in the Northwest: The Yaqui Indians of Sonora, 1740–1976." In *Riot, Rebellion, and Revolution: Rural Social Conflict in Mexico*, pp. 141–175. Edited by Friedrich Katz. Princeton, N.J.: Princeton University Press, 1988.

Imaz, José Luis de. *Los que mandan*. Buenos Aires: Editorial Universitaria de Buenos Aires, 1964.

Johnson, John J. *Political Change in Latin America: The Emergence of the Middle Sectors*. Palo Alto, Calif.: Stanford University Press, 1958.

Katz, Friedrich. "Labor Conditions on Haciendas in Porfirian Mexico: Some Trends and Tendencies." *Hispanic American Historical Review* 54 (February 1974): 30–47.

———. "Rural Uprisings in Preconquest and Colonial Mexico." In *Riot, Rebellion, and Revolution: Rural Social Conflict in Mexico*, pp. 65–94. Edited by Friedrich Katz. Princeton, N.J.: Princeton University Press, 1988.

Kicza, John E. *Colonial Entrepreneurs: Families and Business in Bourbon Mexico.* Albuquerque: University of New Mexico Press, 1983.

———. "The Role of the Family in Economic Development in Nineteenth-Century Latin America." *Journal of Family History* 10 (Fall 1985): 235–246.

Kling, Merle. "Taxes on the 'External' Sector: An Index to Political Behavior in Latin America?" *Midwest Journal of Political Science* 3 (May 1959): 127–150.

———. "Towards a Theory of Power and Political Instability in Latin America." *The Western Political Quarterly* 9 (March 1956): 21–35.

Knowlton, Robert J. "La individualización de la propiedad corporativa civil en el siglo xix—notas sobre Jalisco." *Historia mexicana* 28 (julio–septiembre 1978): 24–61.

Kula, Witold. *Economic Theory of the Feudal System.* New York: NLB, 1976.

Kuznesof, Elizabeth, and Robert Oppenheimer. "The Family and Society in Nineteenth-Century Latin America: An Historiographical Introduction." *Journal of Family History* 10 (Fall 1985): 215–234.

Ladd, Doris M. *The Mexican Nobility at Independence 1780–1826.* Austin: Institute of Latin American Studies, University of Texas at Austin, 1976.

Lambert, Jacques. *Latin America: Social Structure and Political Institutions.* Berkeley: University of California Press, 1967.

Laslett, Peter, ed. *Household and Family in Past Time.* Cambridge: Cambridge University Press, 1972.

Lasswell, Harold Dwight, and Abraham Kaplan. *Power and Society.* New Haven, Conn.: Yale University Press, 1950.

Lavrin, Asunción. "The Execution of the Laws of *Consolidación* in New Spain: Economic Aims and Results." *Hispanic American Historical Review* 53 (February 1973): 27–49.

Liehr, Reinhard. "La deuda exterior de Mexico y los 'merchant bankers' británicos, 1821–1860." *Ibero-Amerikanisches Archiv* N.F. 9:3/4 (1983): 415–439.

Lerdo de Tejada, Miguel. *Comercio esterior de México, desde la conquista hasta hoy.* Mexico: R. Rafael, 1853.

Lombardo de Ruiz, Sonia. "Construction and Contractors: A Methodological Approach to the Study of Architectural Styles in Mexico City, 1780–1805." *Latin American Research Review* 10 (1975): 128–129.

López Cámara, Francisco. *La estructura económica y social de México en la época de la Reforma.* 4th ed. Mexico: Siglo Ventiuno Editores, 1976.

Løtz, Jorgen R., and Elliot Morss. "Measuring 'Tax-Effort' in Developing Countries." *Staff Papers* (International Monetary Fund) 14 (1967): 478–497.

McAlister, Lyle N. *The 'Fuero Militar' in New Spain, 1764–1800.* Gainesville: University of Florida Press, 1957.

MacLachlan, Colin M., and Jaime E. Rodríguez O. *The Forging of the Cosmic Race: A Reinterpretation of Colonial Mexico.* Berkeley: University of California Press, 1980.

Macune, Charles W., Jr. *El Estado de México y la Federación mexicana, 1823–1835.* Mexico: Fondo de Cultura Económica, [1978].

Mallon, Florencia E. "Peasants and State Formation in Nineteenth-Century Mexico: Morelos, 1848–1858." *Political Power and Social Theory* 7 (1988): 1–54.

Merkx, Gilbert W. "Recessions and Rebellions in Argentina, 1870–1970." *Hispanic American Historical Review* 53 (May 1973): 285–295.

México, Secretaría de Hacienda. *Memoria,* 1825–1844.

Meyer, Jean. "El ocaso de Manuel Lozada." *Historia mexicana* 18 (abril–junio 1969): 535–568.

———. *Problemas campesinos y revueltas agrarias (1821–1910).* Mexico: SepSetentas, 1971.

———. "La propiedad comunal de la tierra y la cohesión social de los pueblos indígenas mexicanos." *Cuadernos americanos* 149 (noviembre–diciembre 1966): 168–181.

Meyer, Michael C., and William L Sherman. *The Course of Mexican History* 3d ed. New York: Oxford University Press, 1987.

Miranda, José. "El liberalismo mexicano y el liberalismo europeo." *Historia mexicana* 8 (abril–junio 1959): 512–523.

———. "La propiedad comunal de la tierra y la cohesión social de los pueblos indígenas mexicanos." *Cuadernos americanos* 149 (noviembre–diciembre 1966): 169–177.

Molina Enríquez, Andrés. *Esbozo de la historia de los primeros diez años de la revolucíon agraria de México (de 1910 a 1920), hecho a grandes rasgos* 5 vols., 2d ed. Mexico: Museo Nacional de Antropología, Historia y Etnografía, 1937.

Moore, Barrington, Jr. *Social Origins of Dictatorship and Democracy: Lord and Peasant in the Making of the Modern World.* Boston: Beacon Press, 1966.

Mora, José María Luis. *Méjico y sus revoluciones.* 4 vols. Paris: Librería de Rosa, 1836.

Moreno Toscano, Alejandra, and Carlos Aguirre Anaya. "Migrations to Mexico City in the Nineteenth Century: Research Approaches." *Journal of International Studies and World Affairs* 17 (1975): 27–42.

Needler, Martin C. *Political Development in Latin America: Instability, Violence and Evolutionary Change.* New York: Random House, 1968.

Nettl, J. P. "The State as a Conceptual Variable." *World Politics* 20 (July

1968): 559–592.

Niblo, Stephen R., and Laurens B. Perry. "Recent Additions to Nineteenth-Century Mexican Historiography." *Latin American Research Review* 13 (1978): 3–45.

O'Gorman, Edmundo. *México: El trauma de su historia.* Mexico: Universidad Nacional Autónoma de México, 1977.

———. *Seis estudios históricos de tema mexicano.* Xalapa: Universidad Veracruzana, 1960.

Olliff, Donathon C. "Mexico's Mid-Nineteenth-Century Drive for Material Development." *Annals of the Southeastern Conference on Latin American Studies* 8 (March 1977): 19–29.

Olson, Mancur, Jr. "Rapid Growth as a Destabilizing Force." *Journal of Economic History* 23 (December 1963): 529–552.

Otero, Mariano. *Ensayo sobre el verdadero estado de la cuestión social y política que se agita en la República mexicana.* Mexico: Ignacio Cumplido, 1842.

Parcero López, María de la Luz. *Lorenzo de Zavala, fuente y orígen de la reforma liberal en México.* Mexico: INAH, 1969.

Parkes, Henry Bamford. *A History of Mexico.* Boston: Houghton Mifflin, 1938.

Perry, Laurens Ballard. *Juárez and Díaz: Machine Politics in Mexico.* DeKalb: Northern Illinois University Press, 1978.

Peza, Juan de Díos. "Entrada del Ejército Trigarante á México." In *Episodios históricos de la Guerra de Independencia,* pp. 301–307. Mexico: "El Tiempo," 1910.

Pimentel, Francisco. *Obras completas de D. Francisco Pimentel. Vol. 3: Memoria sobre las causas que han originado la situación actual de la raza indígena de México y medios de remediarla.* Mexico: Tipografía Económica, 1903.

Porter, Theodore M. *The Rise of Statistical Thinking, 1820–1900.* Princeton, N.J.: Princeton University Press, 1986.

Potash, Robert A. "Historiography of Mexico Since 1821." *Hispanic American Historical Review* 40 (1960): 383–424.

———. *Mexican Government and Industrial Development in the Early Republic: The Banco de Avío.* Amherst: University of Massachusetts Press, 1983.

Powell, T. G. *El liberalismo y el campesinado en el centro de México (1850 a 1876).* Mexico: SepSetentas, 1974.

Priestley, Herbert Ingram. *José de Gálvez, Visitor-General of New Spain.* Berkeley: University of California Press, 1916.

———. *The Mexican Nation, A History.* New York: Macmillan, 1924.

Prieto, Guillermo. *Memorias de mís tiempos.* 2 vols. Mexico: Vda. de Ch. Bouret, 1906.

Putnam, Robert D. *The Comparative Study of Political Elites.* Englewood

Cliffs, N.J.: Prentice-Hall, 1976.

Raat, W. Dirk, ed. *Mexico, from Independence to Revolution, 1810–1910.* Lincoln: University of Nebraska Press, 1982.

Reina, Leticia. *Las rebeliones campesinas en México (1819–1906).* Mexico: Siglo Veintiuno Editores, 1980.

Reyes Heroles, Jesus. *El liberalismo mexicano.* 3 vols. Mexico: UNAM, 1957–1961.

Ridker, Ronald C. "Discontent and Economic Growth." *Economic Development and Cultural Change* 11 (October 1962): 1–15.

Robinson, Joan. *Economic Philosophy.* Harmondsworth, Eng.: Penguin, 1978.

Rodríguez O., Jaime E. *Down from Colonialism.* Introduction by Robert Moreno de los Arcos. Chicano Studies Research Center Publications, no. 3. Los Angeles: University of California, 1983.

———. "Oposición a Bustamante." *Historia mexicana* 20 (octubre–diciembre 1970): 199–234.

Roe, Alan R. "Determinants of Government Revenue Share in Poorer Africa Countries—A Comment." *Economic Journal* 78 (June 1968): 479–481.

Rosa, Luis de la. *Observaciones sobre varios puntos concernientes a la administración pública del estado de Zacatecas.* Baltimore: J. Murphy y Cía., 1851.

Safford, Frank. "The Bases of Political Alignment in Early Republican Spanish America." In *New Approaches to Latin American History,* pp. 71–111. Edited by Richard Graham and Peter H. Smith. Austin: University of Texas Press, 1974.

———. "Politics, Ideology and Society in Post-Independence Spanish America," *The Cambridge History of Latin America,* v. 3, *From Independence to c. 1870.* Cambridge: Cambridge University Press, 1985.

Salvucci, Richard J. "Aspects of United States-Mexico Trade, 1825–80: A Preliminary Survey." Paper presented at the annual meeting of the American Historical Association, Chicago, 1986.

Samponaro, Frank N. "La alianza de Santa Anna y los federalistas, 1832–1834: su formación y desintegración." *Historia mexicana* 30 (enero–marzo 1981): 358–390.

———. "The Political Role of the Army in Mexico, 1821–1848." Ph.D. dissertation, State University of New York at Stony Brook, 1974.

———. "Santa Anna and the Abortive Anti-federalist Revolt of 1833 in Mexico." *The Americas* 40 (July 1983): 95–107.

Sanders, David. *Patterns of Political Instability.* New York: St. Martin's Press, 1981.

Santoni, Pedro. "A Fear of the People: The Civic Militia of Mexico in

1845." *Hispanic American Historical Review* 68 (May 1988): 268–288.

Schneider, Jürgen. *Frankreich und die Unabhängigkeit Spanisch-Amerikas: zum französischen Handel mit den entstehenden Nationalstaaten (1810–1850).* 2 vols. Stuttgart: Klett-Cotta, 1981.

Searing, Donald D. "The Comparative Study of Elite Socialization." *Comparative Political Studies* 1 (January 1969): 471–500.

Shaw, Frederick. "The Artisan in Mexico City, 1824–1853." In *El trabajo y los trabajadores en la historia de México*, pp. 399–418. Compiled by Elsa Cecelia Frost, Michael C. Meyer, and Josefina Zoraida Vázquez. Mexico: El Colegio de México and University of Arizona Press, 1979.

———. "Poverty and Politics in Mexico City, 1824–1854." Ph.D. dissertation, University of Florida, 1975.

Shiels, W. Eugene. "Church and State in the First Decade of Mexican Independence." *Catholic Historical Review* 28 (July 1942): 206–228.

Sierra, Justo. *The Political Evolution of the Mexican People.* Translated by Charles Ramsdell. Austin: University of Texas Press, 1969

Silvert, Kalman H. *The Conflict Society: Reaction and Revolution in Latin America.* New Orleans: Hauser Press, 1961.

Simpson, Lesley Byrd. *Many Mexicos.* New York: G. P. Putnam's Sons, 1941.

Sims, Harold D. *Descolonización en México. El conflicto entre mexicanos y españoles (1821–1831).* Mexico: Fondo de Cultural Económica, 1982.

———. *La expulsión de los españoles de México (1821–1828).* Mexico: Fondo de Cultural Económica, 1974.

Sinkin, Richard N. "The Mexican Constitutional Congress, 1856–1857: A Statistical Analysis." *Hispanic American Historical Review* 53 (February 1973): 1–26.

———. *The Mexican Reform, 1855–1876: A Study in Liberal Nation-Building* (Austin: University of Texas Press, 1979)

Skocpol, Theda. "Explaining Revolutions: In Quest of a Social-Structural Approach." In *Uses of Controversy in Sociology*, pp. 155–175. Edited by Lewis A. Coser and Otto N. Larsen. New York: Free Press, 1976.

———. *States and Social Revolutions: A Comparative Analysis of France, Russia, and China.* Cambridge: Cambridge University Press, 1979.

Smith, Peter H. *Labyrinths of Power: Political Recruitment in Twentieth-Century Mexico.* Princeton, N.J.: Princeton University Press, 1979.

Smith, Robert S. "The Institution of the Consulado in New Spain." *Hispanic American Historical Review* 24 (February 1944): 62–85.

———. "Sales Taxes in New Spain, 1575–1770." *Hispanic American Historical Review* 18 (February 1948): 2–37.

SPSS, Inc., *SPSSX: User's Guide.* 2d ed. Chicago: SPSS, 1986.

Staples, Anne, *La iglesia en la primera república federal mexicana.* Mexico:

SepSetentas, 1976.

Stigler, Stephen M. *The History of Statistics: The Measurement of Uncertainty before 1900.* Cambridge, Mass.: Belknap Press of Harvard University Press, 1986.

Stevens, Donald F. "Economic Fluctuations and Political Instability in Early Republican Mexico." *Journal of Interdisciplinary History* 16:4 (Spring 1986): 645–665.

Stokes, William S. "Violence as a Power Factor in Latin-American Politics." *Western Political Quarterly* 5 (1952): 445–468.

Tanzi, Vito, and Clayton McCuistion. "Determinants of Government Revenue Share among Less-developed Countries: A Comment." *Economic Journal* 77 (June 1967): 403–405.

Taylor, William B. *Drinking, Homicide, and Rebellion in Colonial Mexican Villages.* Stanford, Calif.: Stanford University Press, 1979.

———. *Landlord and Peasant in Colonial Oaxaca.* Stanford, Calif.: Stanford University Press, 1972.

Tenenbaum, Barbara A. "Merchants, Money and Mischief: The British in Mexico, 1821–1862." *The Americas* 35 (January 1979): 317–340.

———. *The Politics of Penury: Debt and Taxes in Mexico, 1821–1856.* Albuquerque: University of New Mexico Press, 1986.

Tornel y Mendívil, José María. *Breve reseña histórica de los acontecimientos mas notables de la Nación mexicana desde el año de 1821 hasta nuestros días.* Mexico: Imprenta de Cumplido, 1852.

Tutino, John M. *From Insurrection to Revolution in Mexico: Social Bases of Agrarian Violence, 1750–1940* (Princeton, N.J.: Princeton University Press, [1986]).

———. "Life and Labor on North Mexican Haciendas." In *El trabajo y los trabajadores en la historia de México*, pp. 339–378. Compiled by Elsa Cecelia Frost, Michael C. Meyer, and Josefina Zoraida Vázquez. Mexico: El Colegio de México and University of Arizona Press, 1979.

———. "Provincial Spaniards, Indian Towns, and Haciendas: Interrelated Agrarian Sectors in the Valleys of Mexico and Toluca, 1750–1810." In *Provinces of Early Mexico: Variants of Spanish American Regional Evolution.* Edited by Ida Altman and James Lockhart. Los Angeles: University of California Press, 1976.

United States, Department of Commerce. *Historical Statistics of the United States from Colonial Times to 1970.* 2 vols. Washington, D.C.: U.S. Government Printing Office, 1975.

Valadés, José C. *Alamán, estadista e historiador.* Mexico: José Porrúa e Hijos, 1938.

———. *Orígenes de la República mexicana, la aurora constitucional.* Mexico:

Editores Mexicanos Unidos, 1972.

———. *Santa Anna y la guerra de Téjas*. Mexico: Editores Unidos Mexicanos, 1965.

Vázquez, Josefina Zoraida. "Los Años Olvidados." *Mexican Studies/Estudios Mexicanos*. 5:2(Summer 1989): 313–326.

Vázquez de Knauth, Josefina. *Mexicanos y norteamericanos ante la Guerra de 47*. Mexico: SepSetentas, 1970.

Velázquez, María del Carmen. *El estado de guerra en Nueva España, 1760–1808*. Mexico: El Colegio de México, 1950.

Voss, Stuart F. *On the Periphery of Nineteenth-Century Mexico: Sonora and Sinaloa, 1810–1877*. Tucson: University of Arizona Press, 1982.

Walker, David W. *Kinship, Business, and Politics: The Martínez del Rio Family in Mexico, 1823–1867*. Austin: University of Texas Press, 1986.

Weaver, Frederick Stirton. "Political Disintegration and Reconstruction in 19th Century Spanish America: The Class Basis of Political Change." *Politics and Society* 5 (1975): 161–183.

Weber, David J. *The Mexican Frontier, 1821–1846: The American Southwest Under Mexico*. Albuquerque: University of New Mexico Press, 1982.

———. "Turner, the Boltonians, and the Borderlands." *American Historical Review* 91 (February 1986): 66–81.

Wolf, Eric R. "The Mexican Bajío in the Eighteenth Century." In *Synoptic Studies of Mexican Culture*, pp. 180–199. New Orleans: Middle American Research Institute, Tulane University, 1957.

Wolf, Eric R., and Edward C. Hansen. "*Caudillo* Politics: A Structural Analysis." *Comparative Studies in Society and History* 9 (January 1967): 168–179.

Zamacois, Niceto de. *Historia de Méjico, desde sus tiempos mas remotos hasta nuestros dias*. 22 vols. Barcelona and Mexico: J. F. Parres, 1880.

Zarco, Francisco. *Historia del Congreso Extraordinario Constituyente de 1856–1857*. 5 vols. Mexico: Talleres de "La Ciencia Jurídica," 1898–1901. Re-edition: Mexico City: El Colegio de Mexico, 1956.

Zavala, Lorenzo de. *Juicio imparcial sobre los acontecimientos de México en 1828–1829*. New York: C. S. Van Winkle, 1830.

———. *Obras. El historiador y el representante popular: Ensayo crítico de las revoluciones de México desde 1808 hasta 1830*. Mexico: Editorial Porrúa, 1969.

Zavala, Silvio, and José Miranda. "Instituciones indígenas en la colonia." *Métodos y resultados de la política indigenista en México. Memorias del Instituto Nacional Indigenista* 6 (1954): 29–112.

Index

About the Author
Donald Fithian Stevens is Associate Professor
in the Department of History and Politics
at Drexel University.

Library of Congress Cataloging-in-Publication Data
Stevens, Donald Fithian, 1953–
Origins of instability in early republican Mexico / Donald Fithian
Stevens.
p. cm.
Includes bibliographical references and index.
ISBN 0-8223-1136-4 (cloth) : $29.95
1. Mexico—Politics and government—1821–1861.   2. Political
stability—Mexico—History—19th century.   I. Title.
F1232.S74   1991
320.972—dc20   90-25357 CIP